NEW CRAFTS

BOOKWORKS

NEW CRAFTS
BOOKWORKS

MARY MAGUIRE

PHOTOGRAPHY BY PETER WILLIAMS

LORENZ BOOKS

FIRST PUBLISHED IN 2000 BY
LORENZ BOOKS

LORENZ BOOKS IS AN IMPRINT OF
ANNESS PUBLISHING LIMITED
HERMES HOUSE
88–89 BLACKFRIARS ROAD
LONDON SE1 8HA

THIS EDITION PUBLISHED IN THE USA BY
LORENZ BOOKS, ANNESS PUBLISHING INC.,
27 WEST 20TH STREET, NEW YORK,
NY 10011; (800) 354-9657

THIS EDITION DISTRIBUTED IN CANADA BY
RAINCOAST BOOKS
8680 CAMBIE STREET
VANCOUVER
BRITISH COLUMBIA V6P 6M9

A CIP CATALOGUE RECORD FOR THIS BOOK IS
AVAILABLE FROM THE BRITISH LIBRARY

ISBN 0-7548-0446-1

PUBLISHER: JOANNA LORENZ
PROJECT EDITORS: EMMA CLEGG AND
        CHARLOTTE BERMAN
PHOTOGRAPHER: PETER WILLIAMS
STYLIST: GEORGINA RHODES
STEP PHOTOGRAPHER: RODNEY FORTE
DESIGNER: LILIAN LINDBLOM
ILLUSTRATORS: MADELEINE DAVID AND
        ROBERT HIGHTON
PRODUCTION CONTROLLER: JOANNA KING

PRINTED AND BOUND IN HONG KONG / CHINA

10 9 8 7 6 5 4 3 2 1

CONTENTS

INTRODUCTION

B OOKBINDING IS AN ANCIENT PRACTICE THAT HAS DEVELOPED INTO A MODERN ART AND A PRACTICAL CRAFT. BOOKBINDING CAN ENHANCE AND TRANSFORM A SEEMINGLY DULL COVER, AND ACT AS A SOURCE OF INSPIRATION FOR CREATING PERSONALIZED ALBUMS AND RECORD BOOKS.

CLEAR INSTRUCTIONS AND STEP-BY-STEP PICTURES GUIDE YOU THROUGH THE 25 PROJECTS, WHICH BECOME GRADUALLY MORE COMPLEX AS THE BOOK PROGRESSES. THE MATERIALS AND EQUIPMENT SECTIONS DESCRIBE EXACTLY WHAT YOU WILL NEED TO MAKE A RANGE OF DISTINCTIVE BOOKS AND ALBUMS.

THE DEVELOPMENT OF BOOKBINDING FROM THE PURELY FUNCTIONAL TO AN ART FORM IN ITS OWN RIGHT IS EXPLORED IN THE HISTORY SECTION, AND THE GALLERY SECTION CONTAINS A SELECTION OF STUNNING EXAMPLES OF BOOK-BINDING DESIGNS AND STYLES OF THE LATTER PART OF THE 20TH CENTURY.

THIS COMBINATION OF DETAILED ADVICE AND BEAUTIFUL IMAGES CANNOT FAIL TO INSPIRE YOU TO CREATE YOUR OWN FABULOUS BOOKS AND ALBUMS TO TREASURE FOREVER.

Left: Bookbinding only requires the use of basic materials and tools, making it simple to create a wide range of books and albums.

HISTORY OF BOOKBINDING

THE WORD "BOOK" DERIVES FROM "BOC", AN OLD ENGLISH WORD MEANING "WRITTEN SHEET". ANCIENT PEOPLES HAD BEEN WRITING THINGS DOWN IN VARIOUS WAYS FOR THOUSANDS OF YEARS, BUT IT WAS THE ANCIENT ROMANS WHO INVENTED THE FIRST BOUND BOOK, OR CODEX, AS THEY CALLED IT. THEY USED STYLI TO WRITE ON WAX-COVERED WOODEN TABLETS WHICH THEY BOUND TOGETHER AT THE SIDES WITH LEATHER THONGS.

During the 2nd century BC, the peoples of Africa, Europe and Asia began using animal hide to make the pages for books. Parchment was developed by the people of Asia Minor using a process which involved soaking goat and sheep hides in water, covering them in lime, and then scraping away the remains of hair and tissue. Finally, the clean hides were stretched over wooden frames and left to dry and bleach in the sun. Bleaching was also achieved using the application of chalk or lime. About twelve sheepskins were needed to make a single book of 150 pages.

The Chinese were the first to practise paper making, which they developed during the 1st century AD. They soaked hemp, mulberry, bamboo, tree bark or rags in water, and then pounded the mixture to form a pulp. A wire mesh tray was dipped into the vat to gather up the pulp and the water was allowed to drain off. The pulp was then pressed and dried. By the 5th century AD, Chinese writers were using paper, which they folded accordion-style to form books.

In time, paper making spread from China; indeed, during the Arab conquest, captive Chinese taught the art to the Arabs, with the result that between the 7th and 12th centuries AD cities such as Damascus and Baghdad became great centres of book production. The Islamic

Right: A 10th century book cover of the Sion Gospels. This stunning example of early German bookbinding is made of wood, and has a gold embossed overlay studded with precious jewels.

held in wooden handles. This technique was first used in the 5th century and is still used to this day. In a technique known as "blind tooling", the tool is heated and then pressed into the leather to leave an impression. Another decorative technique, "gold tooling", involves pressing the tool into gold leaf and "glaire" (a mixture of

Left: A Girdle book. This book was used in Europe in the Middle Ages; the owner would tuck the knot at the side into his girdle or belt so that he would not lose the book when he wasn't reading it.

Below: An enamelled pocket book. This book was also designed to be tied to the owner's belt, this time by means of the metal loops on the top.

Arab Empire enjoyed a high literacy rate, with one in five Arabs being able to read.

It took until the 12th century AD for the art of paper making to spread to the West and even then it was distrusted by many; in some parts of medieval Europe, anything written on paper had no legal standing. During the Middle Ages, bookbinders were patronized by royalty, wealthy private patrons and the Church. Monks were particularly prolific book-binders, most of their books being produced for use in the monasteries. The parchment pages of these books, which bore beautiful illuminated text, were stitched together and laced into wooden boards to keep the parchment flat. The books were generally leather bound, but sometimes so-called "treasure bindings" were worked in gold and silver and elaborately decorated with jewels. Emperors of the Byzantine era even paraded in public processions their most sumptuously decorated books as ostentatious displays of their wealth.

Leather bindings were often decorated using tools made from engraved brass dyes

Above: An embroidered prayer book and bag incorporating gold and silver thread

Right: Sir Julius Caesar's Travelling Bookcase, circa 1620.

vinegar and egg (which helps the gold to stick), before pressing it on to the leather.

The spines of books were not decorated prior to the 16th century, since books were stored either flat or on a shelf with the fore edge facing outwards. It was therefore not until the 17th century that titles and authors' names were tooled on to the spine.

The advent of the printing press meant that smaller, lighter and cheaper books could be produced. The pocket book, developed in Italy in 1507, was so popular that it soon spread across Europe. By the 16th century most books were printed on paper, and bookbinding had developed both structurally and

decoratively. Panel and roll stamped decoration replaced the more time-consuming
tooling techniques.

The Industrial Revolution forced a split
in the bookbinding trade. On the one
hand, there were mechanized workshops
which were able to produce low-cost
books bound in cloth, paper or leather to
meet the growing demands of an
increasingly literate population; on the
other, there were small craft workshops
which continued to produce unique bindings in the traditional manner. The latter
were generally small establishments, run
by a qualified binder assisted by a couple
of apprentices and a journeyman
(a qualified binder unable to afford his
own premises).

Throughout the history of bookbinding,
a huge range of materials has been used to
make and decorate book covers, including
leather, papier-mâché, embroidered
canvas, tortoiseshell, ivory and elaborate
gold and silver work. For the
contemporary bookbinder, the choice is
greater still: diverse synthetic materials
are available, spanning a broad range of
textures, colours and properties.

The hand-binding techniques used
today are much the same as those used by
16th-century hand binders. However, in
recent times, the traditional concepts of
book cover design have given way to
freedom of artistic expression, and today
bookbinders' creations may be regarded as
works of art in themselves.

Above: A 19th-century Persian book with a painted and lacquered binding.

Left: A selection of Art Deco bindings. These brightly-coloured books are now valuable collector's items.

GALLERY

THE NOTION THAT THE BINDING OF A BOOK SHOULD REFLECT THE ESSENCE OF ITS CONTENTS IS A RECENT ONE, AND ONE THAT INSPIRES CONTEMPORARY BINDERS TO CREATE BINDINGS THAT CHALLENGE BOOKBINDING CONVENTIONS. THESE BOOKBINDERS INCORPORATE ALL KINDS OF MODERN MATERIALS AND TEXTURES IN THEIR DESIGNS TO CREATE BOOKS THAT ARE ALMOST ARCHITECTURAL OR SCULPTURAL, AND ARE WORKS OF ART IN THEIR OWN RIGHT.

Right: VIKRAM AND THE VAMPIRE or TALES OF HINDU DEVILRY
The covering leather of this book is black goatskin over an underlayer of white kid glove leather decorated with leather dyes sprayed through stencils and various mesh screens. Inlays are of snakeskin, metallic-surfaced leather and acrylic cabochons.
TREVOR JONES, 1993

Below: MOMENTS OF FORCES
These books use French folded graph paper for the interior, with machine-sewn plastic ribbed sleeves for the cover and hand-drawn inside-the-body images and wireframe computer drawings. Both the covers and the sewing at the spine are reinforced with sheets of printmaking paper offcuts.
SUSAN JOHANKNECHT, 1997

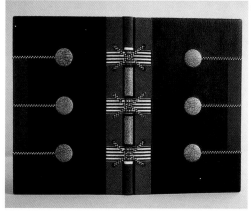

Left: SONGS FROM SHAKESPEARE'S PLAYS
The sewing structure features prominently here. Black goatskin on the sides contrasts with strongly coloured onlays. The top edge was first gilt and then sewn with red linen thread to three black-and-white striped tapes through a concertina-fold continuous guard.
TREVOR JONES, 1995

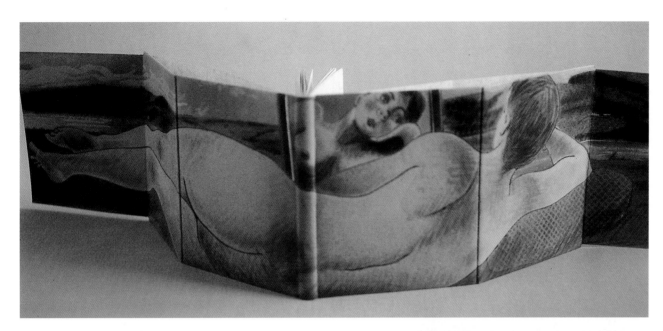

Left: POMES PENYEACH
by James Joyce, 1927
This single-section book
was sewn through the
original three sewing holes
on to a stub, then
endpapers of handmade
paper, dyed to match the
text paper, were added.
The covering leather is
archival natural calfskin
decorated with spirit dyes,
using stencils and resists.
TREVOR JONES, 1991

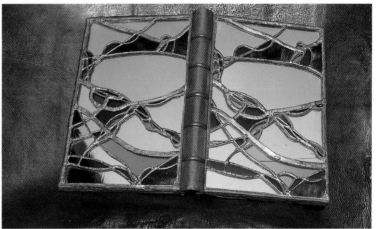

Left: THE SILMARILLION
by J.R.R. Tolkien, 1977
Standing on four glass
bead-headed pins, the
peaks of this book are
integral with the covers,
simply being extended
above the book. The
covers are built from
millboard, balsawood, thin
wooden dowels and
epoxy-putty modelling
supported by brass rods.
PHILIP SMITH, 1983

Above: STAINED GLASS
BOOK
This piece is made from
stained glass which has
been laminated on to
pieces of mirror. This has
then been laminated on to
board for rigidity. It is
held together by a stout
spine made from goatskin,
which is also used around
the edges, and measures
47 x 33 cm (18½ x 13 in).
GAVIN ROOKLEDGE, 1995

Right: A SELECTION OF BLANK BOOKS
This series of books was made to explore the potential of sewing on to rods. Each section and wooden cover board was sewn on to its own rod before the whole book was assembled using vellum strips across the spine. The combinations shown are made from ebony, brass, pine, mahogany and copper.
PETER JONES, 1996

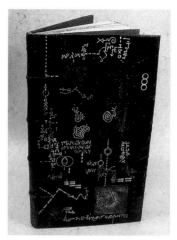

Left: METAMATHICA
Ten sections of D'Arches cover-weight paper were re-sized with gelatine and then with pigments, stainless steel dust and acrylic resin to make this book. Japanese paper was sized, printed and worked in the manner of leather for the spine. The final drawing in white was achieved with airbrush acrylic paint.
TIMOTHY C. ELY, 1990

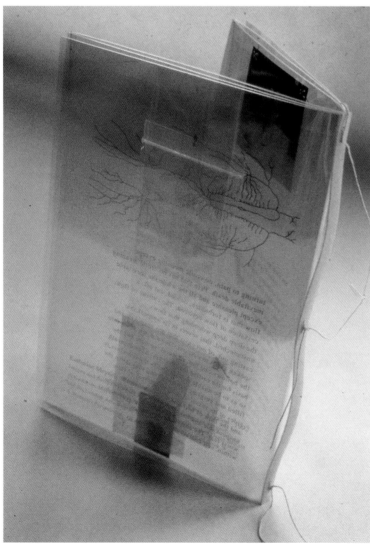

Left: EMISSIONS
A transparent book with all parts observable through the back. Screen-printed on to archival polyester, each copy contains encapsulated transparencies, hair wax, wire and body prints. There are a total of 20 pages sewn into a vellum spine.
SUSAN JOHANKNECHT, 1992

Above: MOBY DICK
by Herman Melville, 1851
This book is bound in black, dark green and dark blue scarph-joined goatskins with various sea-coloured onlays. Most of the surface of the book is built from emulsified maril (a mixture of fine shavings of the grain side of coloured leathers mixed with PVA (white) glue), and modelled with shaped bone folders and card templates.
PHILIP SMITH, 1990

Above: SPANISH LANDSCAPES
This is a full leather binding. The book was sewn on linen tapes laced into boards, then given red silk headbands and a hollow back with one false band which was covered in bright yellow. Natural goatskin was painted with leather dye using an airbrush, brushes and cotton wool. The boards were covered and small onlays of yellow and purple applied. The title was lettered in blind on the lower front board.
SUSAN ALLIX, 1994

Right: HANDS II
(New Testament and Psalms in sculpture)
These life-size hands are made from carved balsawood reinforced with epoxy putty and covered with brown goatskin. The book boards blend into the palms of the hands and fingerprints in ink on light brown acrylic decorate the book edges.
PHILIP SMITH, 1986

Above: THE GARDEN AND OTHER POEMS
by Andrew Marvell
Full leather flexible binding is used with a double cover. The cover is in archival calf leather dyed with blind tooling and then cut into leaf shapes. The fly leaves are made of calf leather with blind tooling imitating the texture of a tree.
EVANGELIA BIZA, 1993

Below: BIRD NESTING
by John Clare, 1987
This book is sewn on three hidden tapes and four visible green-dyed canvas tapes with restraining thongs threaded through eyelets in the sides. The exposed sewing thread is protected by false raised bands of yellow archival goatskin with white acrylic-painted edges.
TREVOR JONES, 1990

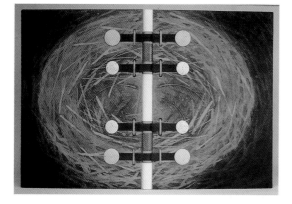

MATERIALS

THE STRUCTURE OF ANY BOOK — THE COVER, PAGES AND BINDING — WILL DETERMINE THE BASIC MATERIALS REQUIRED. FOR THIS REASON THERE ARE SEVERAL STANDARD MATERIALS YOU WILL NEED FOR NEARLY ALL THE PROJECTS IN THIS BOOK: GLUE OR PASTE, PAPER, AND SOME FORM OF CARDBOARD OR BOARD.

BOOKBINDERS' SUPPLIERS PROVIDE MATERIALS SUCH AS ENDPAPERS, BOOK CLOTHS, GLASSINE PAPER AND GLUE. FOR SOME OF THE MORE UNUSUAL PROJECTS YOU WILL NEED TO OBTAIN SPECIFIC MATERIALS, SUCH AS DOLL'S HOUSE WALLPAPER OR CAKE BOARDS, FROM SPECIALIST SHOPS.

Beeswax is used to lubricate linen thread. Pull the thread through the wax to make it glide more easily during stitching.

Book cloth is a paper-backed book-covering cloth, available from specialist bookbinders' suppliers. You can make your own book cloth by gluing thin paper to your choice of fabric.

Cake boards are readily available in supermarkets, cake decorating shops and department stores. They make unusual but practical book boards.

Cardboard of all types is useful for bookbinding. Corrugated cardboard is a very flexible material which is available in a range of colours, including metallic colours, from paper suppliers.

Double-sided heavy-duty carpet tape can often be used instead of glue.

Embroidery threads (flosses) come in many colours. Use two or three strands together, or combine different coloured threads to achieve unusual effects.

Endpapers are specially designed sheets of paper which are pasted to the inside of the cover, leaving an additional flyleaf. Wrapping paper and other decorative papers can also be used, but first apply paste to a small scrap to check whether the paper is colourfast, and that it does not stretch too much when wet.

Fabrics of various types can be made into book cloths.

Glassine paper, available from specialist shops, is thin, transparent acid-free paper that is traditionally used between the pages of photograph albums.

Glue sticks are a source of acid-free adhesive for light-weight materials.

Handmade papers are available in a wide range of colours, effects and designs, some with flower and grass inclusions.

Linen tape is available from haberdashers (notions) or specialist supply shops. It is used to reinforce the spine of books.

Linen thread is used to stitch pages. Run the thread through beeswax before stitching, to make it glide through the holes more easily.

Millboard (pasteboard) is an extremely tough and dense board which is available in different grades of thickness. Millboard is ideal for making portfolios, but hardboard is a good alternative.

Moss paper, as its name suggests, is a furry, moss-like paper which makes interesting book covers or endpapers. It is available from model and hobby shops.

Mull is used to reinforce the inside of a book's spine. Open-weave cotton bandage makes an effective substitute.

Neutral PVA (white) glue, or conservation paste, is available from specialist shops. It is acid free and suitable for archive-quality work.

Paper doilies are inexpensive lacy paper decorations. Available from supermarkets and kitchenware shops.

Polyboard (foam board) is a smooth lightweight card (cardboard). It cannot be folded, but makes a strong book cover.

Polypropylene is a type of flexible plastic used for making book covers. It is available in a wide range of colours.

Self-adhesive cloth tape is book cloth with a self-adhesive backing. Doubled back on itself, it makes a neat, strong tab.

Two-part epoxy glue, or epoxy resin glue, dries very quickly, so prepare only a small quantity at a time. It takes about 24 hours to set but, once set, it makes an excellent bond.

Wallpaper paste can be mixed with PVA (white) glue to produce a strong, slippery glue that allows for repositioning before the paste becomes too tacky.

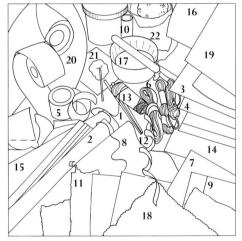

KEY
1 Beeswax	**11** Handmade papers
2 Book cloth	**12** Linen tape
3 Cake boards	**13** Linen thread
4 Cardboard	**14** Millboard (pasteboard)
5 Double-sided heavy-duty carpet tape	**15** Moss Paper
6 Embroidery threads (flosses)	**16** Mull
	17 Neutral PVA (white) glue
7 Endpapers	**18** Paper doily
8 Fabrics	**19** Polypropylene
9 Glassine paper	**20** Self-adhesive cloth tape
10 Glue Sticks	**21** Two-part epoxy glue
	22 Wallpaper paste

EQUIPMENT

PERHAPS BECAUSE OF ITS ANCIENT ORIGINS, BOOKBINDING DOES NOT REQUIRE A GREAT VARIETY OF TOOLS. MUCH OF THE EQUIPMENT YOU WILL NEED TO COMPLETE THE PROJECTS IN THIS BOOK IS BASIC AND, SHOULD YOU NOT ALREADY OWN IT, READILY AVAILABLE FROM HARDWARE STORES. POWER TOOLS ARE NOT REQUIRED, NOR ARE SPECIALIST SKILLS. THE MORE SPECIALIST TOOLS, SUCH AS DECKLE-EDGED SCISSORS AND BONE FOLDERS, CAN BE OBTAINED FROM BOOK-BINDING SUPPLIERS. TAKE CARE WHEN USING SHARP INSTRUMENTS AND DISPOSE OF ANY USED BLADES SAFELY.

Bone folders are inexpensive and very useful implements for creasing paper and smoothing out the air bubbles on pasted boards. They are available from specialist bookbinding shops. Broad ice cream (popsicle) sticks make a satisfactory alternative.

Bradawls (awls) are used, with a hammer, to make single, fine holes in paper or thin card (cardboard).

Brushes in various sizes are used for spreading glue. After using water-soluble glue, clean and dry the brushes carefully so that you will be able to use them again and again.

Craft knives, some with removable and replaceable blades, are useful for accurate cutting of paper and thin card (cardboard). Handle the blades with extreme caution, and dispose of them safely after use. Always cut on a cutting mat.

Cutting mats (preferably of the self-healing kind) should be used to protect your work surface when cutting paper or boards. You will be able to exert more pressure if you kneel and work on the floor.

Deckle-edged scissors are used to cut fancy edges on paper and thin card (cardboard). They are available in a range of patterns from specialist supply shops.

Leather punches have a selection of punches that punch holes of a corresponding size in fabric and cardboard, as well as leather.

Metal rulers are important for accurate measurement and provide a good edge against which paper or board can be cut with a utility or craft knife. Choose a long ruler if possible.

Pencils are used to mark measurements on paper or board. A sharp pencil (or knitting needle) can also be used to punch a hole in polyboard. The pencil should be swivelled around until the desired hole size is achieved, then the edges of the hole can be trimmed against the pencil tip using a craft knife.

Pinking shears cut a zigzag edge, and can be used in the same way as deckle-edged scissors, to create interesting page edge effects.

Pliers-type paper hole punches are inexpensive tools which are useful for punching holes of a regular size in paper and thin card (cardboard). They have a single punch which allows you to place the holes as you choose.

Punches are used, with a hammer, to make holes in plastic or fabrics.

Rotary cutters are useful for cutting paper. They are low-friction cutting tools, so they exert less drag on the paper than a craft knife.

Tack hammers are used to tap in panel pins, or to tap a bradawl (awl) (to make a hole) or a chisel (to make a slot). A heavier hammer is generally not necessary for bookbinding projects.

Utility knives are used for cutting denser material such as cardboard and millboard. A non-retractable utility knife is probably the safest alternative. Trim the uneven pages of a newly completed book against a metal ruler using a utility knife. Always cut on a cutting mat.

Weights of all types are useful for pressing pasted boards or finished books, to prevent warping while the glue dries. Use cooking weights, fitness training weights or telephone directories, and try to exert an even pressure on the boards. When pressing a finished book, remember to protect the spine.

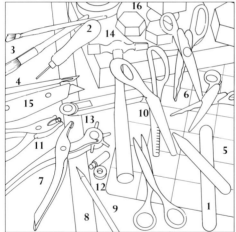

Key

1 Bone folders	**9** Pencil
2 Bradawl (awl)	**10** Pinking shears
3 Brushes	**11** Pliers-type punch
4 Craft knife	**12** Punch
5 Cutting mat	**13** Rotary cutter
6 Deckle-edged scissors	**14** Tack hammer
7 Leather punch	**15** Utility knife
8 Metal ruler	**16** Weights

BASIC TECHNIQUES

Most of the materials used in bookbinding are easy to handle, but before you attempt some of the more complicated projects there are a few techniques that you should make yourself familiar with. Look through this section before starting the projects.

CUTTING TECHNIQUES

Different materials require different cutting techniques and equipment. It is worth learning the appropriate techniques for reasons of speed and safety.

Cutting Board

When cutting a dense material, such as millboard (pasteboard), it is best to cut with a non-retractable craft knife against a metal ruler. Always cut on a protective surface, such as a cutting mat. You will be able to exert more pressure if you kneel and work on the floor.

Cutting Polyboard (Foam Board)

Polyboard has a layer of polystyrene (styrofoam) sandwiched between two layers of laminated card (cardboard). It can be partially cut through to form a hinge. This makes it an easy option for making a book cover.

Partially Cutting Polyboard

1 Using a sharp craft knife and ruler, cut two parallel lines, taking care to cut through the first layer of card (cardboard) and foam but not through the bottom layer.

2 Score corresponding lines on the inside of the card and bend into a book shape so that the cut becomes the spine. This can be reinforced with mull or open-weave bandage.

3 If you want the back to hinge from the spine, as in the Beachcomber's Book, cut another two parallel lines on the opposite side.

4 Score the backs of these lines and fold as shown.

MAKING HOLES

Making a Hole Gauge

Cut a strip of scrap paper or card (cardboard) the exact length of the pages of your book. Measure and mark the position of the holes you need on each page. Align the hole gauge with the spine of the first page, or set of pages, and, using it as your guide, mark the position of the holes on the page. Use it to mark all the pages or sets of pages of the book. Use a bradawl (awl) or bodkin to make the holes.

Making Holes in Paper and Thin Card (Cardboard)

For paper and thin card, a pliers-type hole punch is best. It has a single punch so you can place the holes as you choose.

Making Holes in Polyboard (Foam Board)

1 A sharp, pointed implement, such as a pencil or knitting needle, is best for making holes in polyboard.

2 When the point emerges on the other side of the board, swivel it around until you achieve the desired hole size. Trim the edges against the tip of the pencil or knitting needle using a craft knife.

Making Holes in Heavier Card (Cardboard) and Leather

Use a leather punch with an adjustable head to make holes in thicker card (cardboard) or leather. When working with very dense card, you will have to swivel the board as you press, or try from both sides. It is possible to drill holes, but first drill a test hole in a scrap piece of card.

MAKING ALBUMS

Make allowances for the bulk of the contents of albums by either adding an extra strip of card (cardboard) to the margin, or allowing an extra 2.5 cm (1 in) on the page width and fold this in, as in the Archive Album. Here, the margin is folded in twice. Protect photographs with glassine paper cut slightly smaller than the page and inserted into the folded edge.

MAKING PASTE

PVA (white) glue is a good all-purpose glue, but it grips so efficiently it does not allow for easy repositioning. If you mix it with wallpaper paste in a ratio of 1:1, it will be more slippery and will allow you to reposition the surfaces. It is worth experimenting first, especially if you are using expensive materials.

GLUING AND PASTING BOOK COVERS

1 Use a brush to ensure an even coating. Lay your work on a fresh sheet of scrap paper each time you glue and make sure you spread the glue right to the edge.

2 Line up the paper or book cloth carefully before positioning it. Once in position, smooth with a bone folder, taking care to remove any air pockets.

3 For the spine, carefully cut two parallel slits in the cover to correspond with the edges of the spine. Don't cut right up to the book; allow 2mm/($\frac{1}{16}$ in) for turning. Using a bone folder or similar, tuck in the book cloth overlap at the top and bottom of the spine.

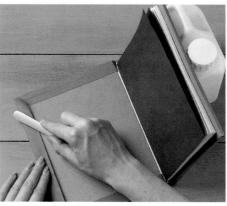

4 Before turning in the edges, cut diagonally across the corners, about 2 mm ($\frac{1}{16}$ in) (or the thickness of the board) from the corners of the board. Pinch the corners with your fingernail or a bone folder before you start to turn the edges in. Turn the top and bottom edges first, then the side edges, and smooth over with a bone folder.

LINING A BOOK COVER

Cut the lining paper to size. Lay the cover, right side down, on a fresh sheet of scrap paper. Apply paste to the inside of the cover, and lay the lining paper on top. Smooth out any creases or air bubbles using a bone folder. Sticky-backed felt can be used as an alternative to paper; in this case, you do not need glue, but take care when you remove the backing, and try to avoid making creases.

MAKING A BOOK CLOTH

Readymade book cloth is available from bookbinders' suppliers (see Suppliers), but it is a simple matter to make your own by lining your choice of fabric with a thin sheet of paper. Simply cut the paper larger than the fabric, spread PVA (white) glue on to the paper and wait until it becomes tacky. Then place the fabric, right side up, on to the glued paper and smooth out any air bubbles using a bone folder. Turn over, smooth the paper and allow to dry.

WEIGHTING OR PRESSING

Weighting Pasted Boards

Pasted boards should be weighted until the glue has dried, to prevent them from warping. First, place a telephone directory on the board to weight it evenly. Then place weights, bricks or other heavy objects on the top.

Weighting a Finished Book

When pressing a finished book, be sure to protect the spine. Sandwich the book between two sheets of cardboard or two telephone directories, allowing the spine to protrude so that the weights do not press on to it.

TRIMMING PAGES

Often when you have made the body of the book, the pages are a little uneven. Trim the edges against a metal cutting ruler, keeping your hand steady and maintaining firm pressure on a utility knife. You may need to make several strokes in order to cut through the bulk of pages.

DECKLE EDGING

All sorts of fancy scissors are available, with patterned cutting edges to give petal effect borders. These patterns work best when paper in subtle and contrasting colours is used, but it is worth experimenting for yourself. Corner cutters are also available.

STITCHING

Traditional bookbinding is a painstaking craft involving several stitching techniques. However, a few simple yet effective stitching methods are all you need to make interesting books. The easiest of these methods, a simple stabbing technique, involves a single stitch passing through folds of paper and a cover, before being tied, as shown in the Precious Pamphlet. A slightly more sophisticated method involves stitching together several groups of pages, as in the Garden Notebook, shown here. In this example, three sets of pages have been stitched alongside each other.

This simple technique can be extended for decorative use. Here, three folded sets of pages have each been stitched three times to achieve an elegant effect.

JAPANESE BINDING

This is both a decorative and functional form of binding. It is an easy way to bind single sheets of paper, as it is the stitching that holds the pages of the book together: gluing is not necessary.

1 After making corresponding holes in the pages with a hammer and bradawl (awl) or punch, line up the pages and hold them securely. Wax the thread before you begin stitching as this makes it easier to pull through the holes.

2 Start the binding by tying a knot in the thread on the inside, near the spine at the bottom of the book.

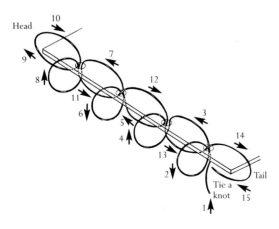

3 Pass the needle on the underside through the first hole, then around the spine and back through the same hole, forming a loop over the back of the spine. Then take the needle down to the next hole, and again around the spine, repeating this pattern until you have reached the last hole. Now take the thread over the top of the book, back through the top hole, then thread in and out of the holes and around the bottom, as shown in the diagram. Conceal the knot on the inside of the cover.

STITCHING WITH RIBBON OR STRING

Other materials, such as thin ribbon or string, can be used for stitching, as long as the holes are big enough. In the Japanese Stork Album, braided string is threaded through the holes using a twisted bit of wire as a guide.

ALL-IN-ONE STITCHING

This method is used for the Classic Notebook and the Triangular Book. It is a moderately difficult technique and the instructions need to be followed carefully.

1 Make a hole gauge on a margin of scrap paper cut to size. Use this to ensure all the holes correspond with each other. Make the holes using a bradawl (awl) or bodkin.

2 To make a "W" fold, take a sheet of folded paper, measure 2.5 cm (1 in) from the centre fold, and fold it back on itself. Return the fold to form a "W" and cut off the remaining paper. This is known as the "wasted edge". Glue the endpaper to the outside edge of the "W". Make two the same.

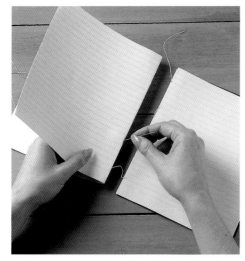

3 Using a long length of linen thread, start stitching through the "W" fold of the last page and endpaper, going in and out of the holes. When you reach the bottom hole, add the next section by stitching through the corresponding hole and continue in running stitch to the top of the book.

4 Once the first section has been attached to the "W" folded endpaper, pull the thread tightly in the direction of the thread, taking care not to tear the holes, and make a double knot.

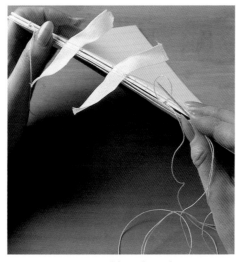

5 Continue to add in the other sections in the same way, binding back under the previous section at the top and bottom through the loop, as shown. Slide two strips of seam binding or linen tape under the stitches across the spine.

6 When all the sections and both endpapers have been bound, knock the spine of the book firmly on the work surface to align the pages.

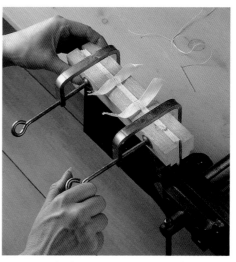

7 Put the body of the book into a vice and clamp two strips of wood in position, one on each side of the spine.

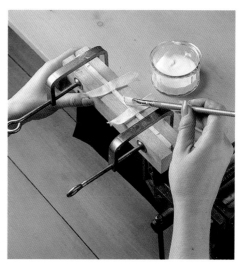

8 Apply neat PVA (white) glue along the spine of the book and place a strip of mull over the top. Apply more glue over the mull.

CD RECORD BOOK

IF YOU WANT TO PERSONALIZE A BOOK BUT DON'T WANT TO GO TO THE BOTHER OF MAKING IT YOURSELF, AN EASIER OPTION IS TO CUSTOMIZE A READYMADE ONE. HERE AN ORDINARY SPIRAL-BOUND BOOK GETS A FUNKY, FUTURISTIC LOOK WITH SILVER SPRAY AND THE ADDITION OF A CD AND SMALL CONVEX MIRROR ON THE FRONT. CDS ARE OFTEN GIVEN AWAY FREE WITH MAGAZINES, AND MAKE AN INEXPENSIVE DECORATION. SELF-ADHESIVE MIRRORS ARE AVAILABLE FROM CAR ACCESSORY SHOPS. USE THIS BOOK TO KEEP NOTES OF YOUR FAVOURITE MUSIC, OR TO KEEP TRACK OF CDS YOU HAVE BORROWED FROM OR LENT TO FRIENDS.

1 Spray the front cover of the book with silver paint. Don't forget to include the side edges. Once dry, turn over and spray the back cover.

2 Attach the mirror to the centre of the CD, so that it covers the central hole.

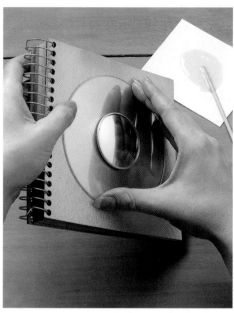

3 Using two-part epoxy glue, glue the CD to the front cover of the book and allow the glue to dry.

MATERIALS AND EQUIPMENT YOU WILL NEED

SPIRAL-BOUND BOOK • SILVER SPRAY PAINT • SMALL CIRCULAR CONVEX SELF-ADHESIVE MIRROR • SPARE CD • TWO-PART EPOXY GLUE

CHILD'S ART BOOK

Many of us keep mounds of our children's artwork, stacked in untidy piles. Instead, why not make a special scrapbook — with your child's help — to protect and display those precious pictures? Let your child design the front and back covers (but first check with your local printer the sizes they are able to bind and laminate), and together you can choose the colours for the inside pages; here we've used bright yellow and orange. Then fill the scrapbook with your favourite pictures.

1 Having checked with your local printer about the appropriate size, let your child paint or draw two pictures, one for front cover and one for the back cover. Trim the pictures if necessary.

2 Lay the coloured card (cardboard) on a cutting mat and, using a craft knife and ruler, cut the card pages to size. Here, the back cover is cut larger than the front cover, and the alternating orange and yellow pages are cut gradually larger, so that the contrasting colours are visible from the front.

3 Collate the scrapbook as desired. Take it to your local printer and ask to have the front and back covers laminated, and have the spine spiral-bound.

MATERIALS AND EQUIPMENT YOU WILL NEED
2 CHILD'S DRAWINGS, OF A SUITABLE SIZE FOR BINDING AND LAMINATING • SCISSORS • 20 SHEETS OF THIN COLOURED CARD (CARDBOARD) •
CUTTING MAT • CRAFT KNIFE • METAL RULER

EXOTIC TRAVELOGUE

WHAT BETTER RECORD OF YOUR TRAVELS THAN A BOOK THAT YOU CAN SEND HOME — SECURED FROM PRYING EYES WITH STRING AND SEALING WAX — TO AWAIT YOUR TRAVEL-WEARY RETURN? THIS IS A SIMPLE PROJECT, USING A READYMADE BOOK WITH BROWN PAGES TO SUIT THE THEME. EVEN IF YOU HAVEN'T TRAVELLED TO DISTANT SHORES, YOU CAN STILL DECORATE THE INTRIGUING "PACKAGE" WITH INTERESTING STAMPS FROM PHILATELISTS' SHOPS.

1 Measure the dimensions of the book and draw on to the brown paper. Make a small extra allowance for wrapping around the corners.

2 Cut two slits down from the top of the paper to meet the marking for the spine. Do the same from the bottom. Fold each strip over at the spine marking and stick down with a glue stick. Fold in a 2 mm (1/16 in) edge on both sides of the gaps. Apply double-sided tape along the spine of the book and stick it on to the reinforced strip of brown paper.

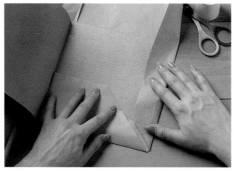

3 Support the book on its spine. Lay open the back cover and wrap it as you would a parcel, using glue or double-sided tape. Repeat for the front cover.

4 Using PVA (white) glue, glue a range of stamps on to the front cover.

5 Tie up the book with string as you would a parcel, then use a match to melt sealing wax on the string at the spine to hold it in place.

MATERIALS AND EQUIPMENT YOU WILL NEED
RULER • PENCIL • THICK NOTEBOOK WITH BROWN PAGES • BROWN PARCEL PAPER • SCISSORS • GLUE STICK • DOUBLE-SIDED CARPET TAPE, SLIGHTLY WIDER THAN THE SPINE OF THE BOOK • PVA (WHITE) GLUE • ASSORTED STAMPS • STRING • BOX OF MATCHES • SEALING WAX

SLATE SKETCHBOOK

THIS EASY-TO-MAKE SKETCHBOOK UTILIZES TWO INEXPENSIVE SLATE DRAWING BOARDS FOR ITS COVERS, ALLOWING YOU TO PRACTISE YOUR ARTWORK BEFORE COMMITTING YOURSELF TO PAPER. THE INSIDE PAGES ARE MADE FROM INDIAN KHADI PAPER IN VARIOUS COLOURS. KHADI PAPER HAS A ROUGH TEXTURE SUITABLE FOR PASTEL AND CHARCOAL WORK, BUT YOU CAN USE WHATEVER PAPER YOU LIKE. THE ELASTIC BINDING ALLOWS FOR EXPANSION, SHOULD YOU WANT TO GLUE BULKY MATERIAL INSIDE, AND IT ALSO ALLOWS THE OPEN BOOK TO LIE FLAT. EXTRA PAGES CAN EASILY BE ADDED IF NECESSARY.

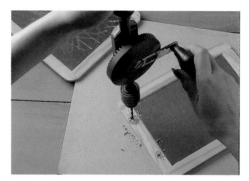

1 Drill two corresponding holes in each slate board, about 6 cm (2½ in) apart.

2 Crease the edges of the paper and tear with a metal ruler to get a deckle-edge effect. Glue two tabs cut from narrow cloth tape on each page, about 4 cm (1½ in) apart, so that the centres of the tabs are 6 cm (2½ in) apart. Fold the tabs so that they stick to both sides of the page. Make a hole in each tab with a hole punch (see Basic Techniques).

3 Thread the elastic through the holes in the back cover board, page tabs and front cover board and tie in a bow at the front.

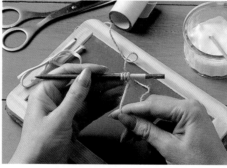

4 Wrap double-sided carpet tape around the top of the slate pencil. Wrap a length of string around the tape, starting at the lower end, and tie in a knot at the top. Glue the knot in place. Tie the free end of the string to the top hole on the back cover board.

5 Lie a piece of wide cloth tape face-down on the frame of the front board, so that it extends over the side. Stick a thinner strip over it, with the sticky sides together, to form the pencil loop. Bring the wide tape over the frame and stick the tape down.

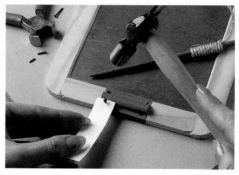

6 Reinforce the loop by gently hammering in panel pins that have been snipped to size. Take care not to split the slate.

MATERIALS AND EQUIPMENT YOU WILL NEED

DRILL • DRILL BIT • 2 SLATE BOARDS • HANDMADE PAPER • METAL RULER • SELF-ADHESIVE CLOTH TAPE, NARROW AND WIDE • SCISSORS • PVA (WHITE) GLUE • HOLE PUNCH • ELASTIC • DOUBLE-SIDED CARPET TAPE • SLATE PENCIL • HEMP STRING • SMALL PANEL PINS • HAMMER

SUEDE DESK PAD

THIS FUNCTIONAL AND STYLISH DESK ACCESSORY IS MADE FROM A RICH RED SUEDE, ALTHOUGH FLAT LEATHER WOULD BE JUST AS EFFECTIVE. IT IS SIMPLY STITCHED AROUND THE EDGE IN A CONTRASTING COLOUR, AND THE SHOELACE AND FEATHER FASTENING GIVES IT AN APPEALING "ANTIQUE" LOOK.

EASY TO MAKE, THIS PROJECT REQUIRES ONLY BASIC SEWING SKILLS FOR THE OVER-STITCHING AND THE PAGE BINDING. LEATHER AND SUEDE SCRAPS CAN BE BOUGHT FROM LEATHER GOODS MANUFACTURERS OR BOOKBINDERS' SUPPLIERS; ALTERNATIVELY, YOU COULD RECYCLE AN OLD BAG OR JACKET.

1 Cut a rectangle of suede or leather and fold in half to check that it is square and even. Mark a 1 cm (½ in) border around the edge, on the wrong side, and punch evenly spaced small holes along this border.

3 In order to punch the marked holes for the stitches, you will need to bunch up the hide into the jaws of the punch. If you are unable to reach the marked positions, use a bradawl (awl) to punch the holes.

5 Divide the paper into three sets. Fold each set in half to mark the spine and mark the stitching holes using a hole gauge (see Basic Techniques). Use a bradawl to punch the holes.

6 Lay the first set of pages down inside the cover. Stitch the pages to the spine of the cover. Do not cut the string once you have stitched this set in place; instead, start stitching the next set. When the three sets of paper are stitched in place, tie a knot in the two ends of the string and tuck the knot out of sight inside the spine. The three lines of stitches on the spine should be parallel and straight. Slip the shoelace under the central set of stitches, as shown. Find a suitable feather with which to finish off.

2 Mark out the spine and the position of three parallel rows of three large stitches.

4 Thread a bodkin with a double length of string. Using the pre-punched holes, overstitch all round the edge of the cover.

MATERIALS AND EQUIPMENT YOU WILL NEED

RULER • PENCIL • SUITABLE PIECE OF SUEDE OR LEATHER • SCISSORS • LEATHER HOLE PUNCH • BRADAWL (AWL) • BODKIN • STRING IN A CONTRASTING COLOUR • GOOD-QUALITY PLAIN WRITING PAPER • SCRAP PAPER • LONG SHOELACE, COLOUR TO MATCH THE STRING • FEATHER

PRECIOUS PAMPHLET

ADD A PERSONAL TOUCH TO A SPECIAL FAMILY OCCASION, SUCH AS A WEDDING OR CHRISTENING, WITH THIS UNIQUE PAMPHLET, MADE FROM BEAUTIFUL HANDMADE PAPER, A WORTHY KEEPSAKE OF ANY HAPPY OCCASION. USE A METALLIC PEN TO WRITE THE NAME OF THE WEDDING COUPLE OR BABY ON THE FRONT COVER AND THE INSIDE PAGES. HERE, PRESSED FLOWERS HAVE BEEN USED TO DECORATE THE FRONT, COMPLEMENTING THE FLOWERS ALREADY INCORPORATED IN THE PAPER. THIS IS THE SIMPLEST TYPE OF BOOK TO MAKE, BEING HELD TOGETHER BY ONE STITCH WHICH IS THEN TIED IN A BOW ON THE SPINE.

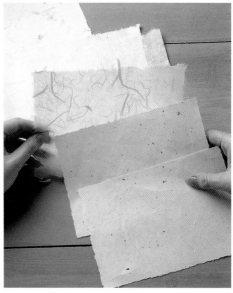

1 Tear the edges of each piece of paper by first creasing it then pulling a metal ruler along the crease to give a natural-looking deckle edge. Vary the sizes of the inner sheets of paper. Collate the pages in order of size, the largest at the back, smallest at the front. Fold in half together to form a booklet.

2 Using a bradawl (awl), make two evenly spaced holes along the spine. Thread the bodkin with a length of raffia and, starting on the outside, make a stitch through the holes, emerging on the outside again. Tie the raffia in a bow on the spine.

3 Glue a small square of paper, the edges torn as before, on the front cover. This is for the name of the baby or wedding couple. Arrange the pressed flowers on the front cover as desired, then glue in place with glue diluted with water.

MATERIALS AND EQUIPMENT YOU WILL NEED
ASSORTED HANDMADE PAPERS, SOME WITH FLOWERS • METAL RULER • BRADAWL (AWL) • BODKIN • RAFFIA •
PVA (WHITE) GLUE • PRESSED FLOWERS

ARTIST'S POCKET BOOK

THIS UNIQUE "POCKET BOOK WITH A POCKET" WOULD MAKE AN IDEAL GIFT FOR A NATURE-LOVING ARTIST. THE WATERCOLOUR PAPER IS FOLDED TO ALLOW FOR A SINGLE, PANORAMIC PAINTING OR SEVERAL SMALLER PAINTINGS, AND A MINIATURE PAINTBOX TUCKS NEATLY INSIDE THE POCKET. NATURAL LINEN IS USED HERE FOR THE COVER BUT A FABRIC SUCH AS VELVET, TEAMED WITH COLOURED PAPER PAGES, WOULD GIVE A MORE EXOTIC FEEL.

1 Cut two rectangles each of polyboard (foam board) and wadding (batting), 11 x 15 cm (4¼ x 5⅞ in). The four rectangles should all be identical.

2 From linen, cut out two identical larger rectangles for the cover. Cut out a smaller square for the pocket to hold the paintbox, plus extra for trimmings. Using the selvedge edge as the top of the pocket, fold in the sides and bottom, shaping it as shown.

3 Pin the pocket to the centre of one linen rectangle. Using running stitch and contrasting embroidery thread (floss), sew the pocket in place, gathering it very slightly to allow for the bulk of the paint-box. Leave the top open. Attach a long piece of tape to the centre of the other linen rectangle, using three cross stitches in a different colour of thread.

4 Stick double-sided tape around the edge on one side of a polyboard rectangle. Sandwich a wadding rectangle between the linen rectangle (linen tape facing down) and the polyboard rectangle (double-sided tape facing up). Stretch the linen over each edge of the rectangle and attach it to the double-sided tape. Trim the corners to reduce the bulk. Repeat for the front cover.

5 Cut or tear (for a deckle-like edge) a long strip of watercolour paper. Using pencil, mark out identical intervals, slightly less than the width of the cover. It is important to be accurate at this stage, or the pages will lie askew. Using a bone folder and metal ruler, score every alternate marking, then turn the paper over, and again score alternate markings.

6 Fold the paper accordion-style, using the scored markings. Using double-sided tape or glue, attach one end of the folded paper to each cover. Press firmly to ensure the paper has fully adhered.

MATERIALS AND EQUIPMENT YOU WILL NEED

CRAFT KNIFE • METAL RULER • CUTTING MAT • POLYBOARD (FOAM BOARD) • WADDING (BATTING) • NATURAL LINEN • SCISSORS • MINIATURE PAINTBOX • PINS • EMBROIDERY THREAD (FLOSS), IN 2 BRIGHT COLOURS • EMBROIDERY NEEDLE • LINEN TAPE • DOUBLE-SIDED CARPET TAPE • EXTRA-LARGE SHEET OF WATERCOLOUR PAPER • PENCIL • BONE FOLDER • PVA (WHITE) GLUE (OPTIONAL)

NEEDLE BOOKLET

THIS IS AN IDEAL FIRST PROJECT AND IS SUITABLE FOR CHILDREN OR ADULTS, SINCE IT IS QUICK AND EASY TO MAKE, REQUIRES ONLY A FEW BASIC SEWING SKILLS AND JUST A FEW SCRAPS OF MATERIAL AND CAN EVEN BE GLUED TOGETHER IF YOU PREFER. THIS CHARMING TRADITIONAL-STYLE NEEDLE BOOKLET WOULD MAKE A LOVELY MOTHER'S DAY GIFT FOR A CHILD TO MAKE WITH JUST A LITTLE SUPERVISION AND GUIDANCE.

1 Using pinking shears, cut two rectangles of green felt, one 14 x 22.5 cm (5½ x 9 in) and one 2 x 22.5 cm (¾ x 9 in) and one of orange felt 8.5 x 11 cm (3⅓ x 4½ in). Cut a rectangle of yellow felt 12.5 x 21 cm (5 x 8⅓ in) with ordinary scissors. Make a flower template and cut out each part of the flower from the remaining felt. Use pinking shears for the leaves and flower centre, and ordinary scissors for the flower head and stem.

2 Using blue embroidery thread (floss) and running stitch, sew the leaves and stem on to the orange rectangle.

3 Using pink thread and running stitch, sew on the flower head. Then position a white felt circle on the centre of the flower and attach by embroidering French knots.

4 Using blue thread and running stitch, sew the orange patch on to one half of the yellow felt rectangle.

5 Sandwich a rectangle of fusible bonding web between the yellow and green felt and iron to bond them. Using pinking shears, cut an orange page 12 x 20 cm (4¾ x 8 in) and a yellow page 10 x 18 cm (4 x 7 in). Place the green strip across the middle of the cover, to make a spine.

6 Place the yellow page on the orange page inside the cover. Using blue thread, work a row of running stitches through all the layers to attach the pages. Finish by sewing a button to the top and bottom of the green felt spine.

MATERIALS AND EQUIPMENT YOU WILL NEED

PINKING SHEARS • FELT: GREEN, ORANGE, YELLOW AND WHITE • SCISSORS • PENCIL • TRACING PAPER • EMBROIDERY NEEDLE • BLUE AND PINK EMBROIDERY THREADS (FLOSSES) • FUSIBLE BONDING WEB • IRON • 2 BUTTONS

BABY'S CLOTH BOOK

A SOFT CLOTH BOOK MAKES A LOVELY PRESENT, AND THIS ONE HAS AN ADDED SURPRISE: A SQUEAKER IS SEWN UNDER THE COVER MOTIF TO DELIGHT AN INQUISITIVE BABY OR TODDLER. THE BOOK CAN BE MADE FROM RECYCLED FABRIC SUCH AS AN OLD BLANKET AND THE APPLIQUÉD CAT FROM AN OUTGROWN BABY OUTFIT, OR YOU CAN MAKE YOUR OWN PICTURES. TRY TO INCORPORATE SEVERAL TEXTURES TO GIVE EXTRA STIMULATION FOR THE BABY. FINALLY, MAKE SURE EVERYTHING IS SECURELY STITCHED, ESPECIALLY THE FRONT MOTIF OVER THE SQUEAKER, SO THAT NOTHING CAN BE PULLED OFF AND SWALLOWED.

1 Using pinking shears, cut pages all the same size from an old blanket. Lay the pages one on top of the other and fold them in half to mark the position of the spine. Lay the pages on the cover fabric and cut out the cover, allowing an extra 5 cm (2 in) on each side. Cut a square of blanket smaller than the front cover to make a patch. Using scissors, cut a motif from an old garment, or design your own, for the front cover.

2 Place the squeaker under the motif, then carefully stitch the motif to centre of the patch of blanket. Stitch the patch to the front cover using decorative running stitches in a contrasting thread.

3 Stitch a motif to the centre of each page. Sew the pages to the cover using running stitch in a contrasting thread. Use a different coloured embroidery thread (floss) for each page.

4 As you stitch the pages one by one to the cover, try to keep the rows of stitching straight, neat and evenly spaced along the spine.

5 The cover is cut larger than the pages to allow for the bulk of the cloth book and the thickness of the spine. Once all the pages have been stitched in place, trim off the excess cover fabric using pinking shears.

MATERIALS AND EQUIPMENT YOU WILL NEED

PINKING SHEARS • OLD BLANKET • SOFT FABRIC FOR THE COVER • SCISSORS • ASSORTED MOTIFS, ONE FOR EACH PAGE AND FRONT COVER •
TOY SQUEAKER • EMBROIDERY NEEDLE • ASSORTED EMBROIDERY THREADS (FLOSSES)

CHILDHOOD MEMORIES BOOK

CHOOSE FABRIC THAT IS EVOCATIVE OF YOUR CHILDHOOD TO MAKE THE COVER OF THIS SPECIAL BOOK. THE LINEN PAGES ALLOW YOU TO STITCH ON A COLLAGE OF ALL THOSE BELOVED THINGS: A PRETTY BUTTON, SCRAP OF LACE OR SWATCH OF FABRIC FROM A DRESS THAT WAS A CHILDHOOD FAVOURITE, OR BELONGED TO YOUR MOTHER OR GRANDMOTHER. ASK YOUR LOCAL PRINT SHOP TO TRANSFER YOUR PHOTOGRAPHS ON TO CLOTH — YOU MAY BE ABLE TO MOUNT PHOTOGRAPHS ON EVERY PAGE. TRY TO AVOID ANYTHING BULKY BUT, APART FROM THAT, THE CHOICE IS AS PERSONAL AS YOUR MEMORIES!

1 Cut cover and lining fabrics 34 x 61 cm (13½ x 24 in). Allow extra for the cover if the pattern needs to be altered to make front and back correspond, as here (the dart in the centre is where the spine will be). Press a 1 cm (½ in) hem on each piece. Cut off the corners to reduce bulk.

2 Pin under the hems. Embroider the appropriate dates on to the wide webbing tape, choosing a thread colour to complement the cover fabric.

3 Tack (baste) the cover and lining hems (dart if applicable). Fray the edges of a cloth photograph and stitch onto the cover using embroidery thread (floss). Add buttons and other features, using different stitches and colours of thread.

4 Cut two straps from the medium-width webbing tape, fold the ends to make a point and stitch down. Stitch a buttonhole on each big enough for the buttons to fit through.

5 Stitch the buttonhole straps an equal distance from the top and bottom on the back of the cover. The straps should lie right side down when the book is closed.

6 Stitch buttons in the corresponding positions on the front cover. Tack the cover and lining together, wrong sides facing. Blanket stitch along the sides and bottom using embroidery thread. ▶

MATERIALS AND EQUIPMENT YOU WILL NEED

FABRIC FOR COVER • FABRIC FOR LINING • SCISSORS • RULER • PINS • IRON • CREAM WEBBING TAPE 4 AND 2 CM (1½ AND ¾ IN) WIDE • ASSORTED EMBROIDERY THREADS (FLOSSES) • EMBROIDERY NEEDLE • TACKING (BASTING) THREAD AND NEEDLE • PHOTOGRAPHS TRANSFERRED TO CLOTH • ASSORTED BUTTONS • MILLBOARD (PASTEBOARD), OR SIMILAR • UTILITY KNIFE • CUTTING MAT • METAL RULER • LINEN FOR PAGES

7 Stitch the dart at the spine (if applicable). Slide a piece of millboard (pasteboard) 28 x 30 cm (11 x 12 in) into each side of the cover.

8 Using embroidery thread, stitch a row of running stitches on each side of the spine to hold the boards in place. Blanket-stitch along the top edge to enclose the millboards and complete the cover.

9 Cut five rectangles of linen, each 30 x 58½ cm (12 x 23 in). Fray about 1 cm (½ in) from each edge. Pull a thread to mark the centre fold line of the first page. Using running stitch, sew it on to one end of a 71 cm (28 in) length of medium-width tape. This leaves a long tail of tape for later use.

10 Place all the folded pages along-side each other. Stitch as many on to the long length of tape as possible, keeping the stitching straight and even.

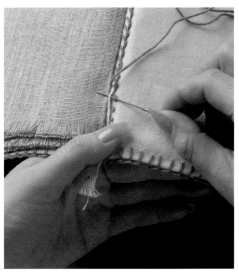

11 Insert the completed pages into the book cover, with the tape in place along the spine. Inside the front cover, oversew the tape to the spine, picking up the running stitch along the spine with the tape edge, as shown. Do the same inside the back cover.

12 Bring the tail of tape on to the spine on the outside of the cover. Tuck the ends under and stitch neatly in place. Hold the tape in place along the spine by sewing a few cross stitches at the top and bottom, pushing the needle through to the tape on the inside.

BEACHCOMBER'S BOOK

Here is a special book in which to store your favourite seashore finds. File the best smooth glass fragments, shells and pebbles in the transparent slide pockets, so that they can be admired from both sides. Sheets of plastic bubble wrap will protect your treasures against breakage, and look far more stylish than one would suppose. A sheet of fused paper evocative of sand and sea is ideal for the cover. If you can't find this type of paper, you can make your own by overlapping two kinds of paper similar to those used here.

1 Cut a rectangle of polyboard (foam board) 23.5 x 62 cm (9⅓ x 24½ in). Mark two parallel lines across the centre, 2.5 cm (1 in) apart. Partially cut through the polyboard along the lines to form the spine (see Basic Techniques).

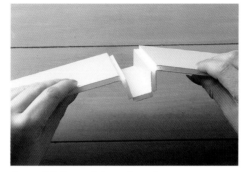

3 Fold the polyboard as shown. Use cloth tape to reinforce the hinge points on the inside, making sure the tape fits right into the cut lines.

5 Using a rotary cutter, cut through the paper on the outside of the cover, along the pre-cut channels in the polyboard spine. (Rotary cutting exerts less drag on paper than a craft knife.)

2 Turn the board over and mark a parallel line 2.5 cm (1 in) on either side of the spine. Partially cut through these lines as before.

4 Cut a piece of seashore-like paper 27.5 x 66 cm (10¾ x 26 in) for the cover and paste this to the outside of the polyboard (see Basic Techniques). Allow the paste to dry.

6 Glue the excess cover paper over onto the inside of the polyboard (see Basic Techniques). Line the inside of the board with more cover paper cut to size. Cut a sandpaper frame for the inside of each cover. ▶

MATERIALS AND EQUIPMENT YOU WILL NEED

CRAFT KNIFE • METAL RULER • CUTTING MAT • POLYBOARD (FOAM BOARD) • SELF-ADHESIVE CLOTH TAPE • SEASHORE-LIKE PAPER • SCISSORS • PASTE (SEE BASIC TECHNIQUES) • ROTARY CUTTER • 2 SHEETS OF COARSE-GRADE SANDPAPER • SLIDE POCKET PAGES • BACKING PAPER • BUBBLE WRAP • NATURAL LINEN THREAD FOR BINDING • LINEN TAPE • BRADAWL (AWL) • PVA (WHITE) GLUE

7 For each page, you will need a slide pocket page, a sheet of backing paper and a piece of bubble wrap, all cut to the right size. Cut three of each layer, then sandwich a slide pocket page between the backing paper and bubble wrap on each page. Using two strips of self-adhesive cloth tape, join the pages down one side. Make three pages in total (if you want more, you can make the spine wider). Fill the pockets with seashore finds.

8 Make small holes at even intervals down the taped edge of each page and bind the three pages in the Japanese style (see Basic Techniques). Push linen tape under the stitches and work into position along the edge of the pages, using a bradawl (awl).

9 Spread PVA (white) glue along the linen tape on the edge.

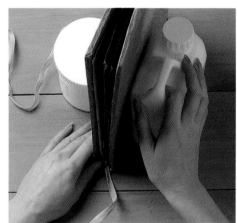

10 Stand the spine of the cover on the work surface and place the glued and bound edge of the pages in position. Support the book while the glue dries. Tie the linen tape in a bow on the outside of the spine.

ROMANTIC KEEPSAKE

TRANSFORM THE COVER OF AN ORDINARY HARD-BACKED DRAWING BOOK WITH CLAY AND BEADS. THE LITTLE SHAPES AND FIGURES ARE STAMPED OUT OF POLYMER CLAY WHICH IS FIRST COATED WITH METALLIC POWDERS. THE SHAPES ARE SIMPLY GLUED IN PLACE ON THE COVER, THEN GLASS BEADS ARE SPRINKLED OVER THE TOP. THE WHOLE BOOK IS THEN BAKED TO SET THE CLAY. THIS LITTLE BOOK IS THE PERFECT PLACE FOR PERSONAL OBSERVATIONS, DIARY ENTRIES OR THOSE PRIVATE AFFAIRS OF THE HEART. MAKE SURE YOU KEEP IT SAFELY STOWED AWAY UNDER LOCK AND KEY!

1 Roll out the polymer clay on a pastry board to a thickness of 4 mm (⅛ in). Wearing a dust mask, paint the surface of the clay with metallic powders to create a variegated effect. Apply two bands of colour and blend them where they meet, using a paintbrush.

2 Stamp out the desired shapes. Smooth rounded edges with your fingertips.

3 Make markings on the shapes using a blunt instrument, such as a clay marking tool or darning needle.

4 Cut border strips from gold-covered polymer clay. Spread glue thickly all over the front of the book and press each shape in place. Stick on the gems and push tiny gems into the clay to make "eyes". Use a dot of glue to stick clay on clay.

5 Liberally sprinkle beads over the remaining glued area. Tie the book closed with string or lightly clamp it shut, then bake it, following the polymer clay manufacturer's instructions.

6 Leave the book to cool, then shake off any loose beads. Apply a coat of varnish to each clay shape.

MATERIALS AND EQUIPMENT YOU WILL NEED

ROLLING PIN • PASTRY BOARD • 2 BLOCKS POLYMER CLAY • DUST MASK • ARTIST'S PAINTBRUSHES • ASSORTED METALLIC POWDERS • ASSORTED SMALL BISCUIT (COOKIE) CUTTERS • CLAY MARKING TOOL, OR DARNING NEEDLE • EPOXY GLUE • FAKE GEMS • TINY GLASS BEADS • STRING OR CLAMP • VARNISH AND BRUSH

CLOUD PILLOW BOOK

THIS SOFT, BILLOWING CLOUD BOOK WILL TUCK NICELY UNDER YOUR PILLOW, WAITING FOR YOU TO FILL ITS PAGES WITH THE REMNANTS OF YOUR DREAMS. USE SILVER INK TO COMPLEMENT THE BLUE PAGES AND TO MATCH THE SILVER ELASTIC BINDING. BOOKS DON'T HAVE TO HAVE THE USUAL FOUR RIGHT-ANGLED CORNERS — THINK OF OTHER INTERESTING SHAPES TO SUIT VARIOUS THEMES, THEN DESIGN AND MAKE YOUR OWN BOOKS.

1 Make a cloud template and draw two cloud shapes on to polyboard (foam board) or card (cardboard). Cut out the clouds using a craft knife.

3 Lay a wadding cloud on top of a polyboard cloud, then stretch the corresponding fleecy cloud over and fix over the edge using double-sided carpet tape. Trim off any bulky areas of fleece.

5 Use the template to cut 20 cloud pages from cloud-effect paper. Punch six holes on the straight edge of each page with a hole punch and strengthen each hole with a ring reinforcer.

2 Using the cloud template cut out two wadding (batting) and two felt clouds. Cut two more clouds from fleecy fabric, allowing an excess of 1.5 cm (⅝ in) all around. Cut the fleecy cloud for the back cover in reverse, so that the fleece is on the outside.

4 Lay a sticky-backed felt cloud over the unfinished side of each cloud, then carefully remove the backing and smooth out any creases.

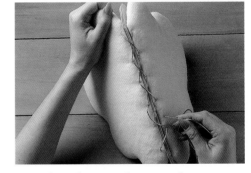

6 Place the pages between the covers. Using silver elastic and a bodkin, stitch through the padding (but not the polyboard) and the holes, making diagonal stitches. Work back up the spine, crossing over the first row of stitches with stitches in the opposite direction.

MATERIALS AND EQUIPMENT YOU WILL NEED

PENCIL • PAPER • SCISSORS • POLYBOARD (FOAM BOARD) OR CARD (CARDBOARD) • CRAFT KNIFE • CUTTING MAT • WADDING (BATTING) • WHITE STICKY-BACKED FELT • CREAM FLEECY FABRIC • DOUBLE-SIDED CARPET TAPE • CLOUD-EFFECT BLUE PAPER, A4 SIZE (8½ X 11 IN) • HOLE PUNCH • WHITE SELF-ADHESIVE RING REINFORCERS • SILVER CORD ELASTIC • BODKIN

GARDEN NOTEBOOK

THIS USEFUL BOOK WOULD MAKE A WONDERFUL PRESENT FOR A FRIEND OR RELATIVE WHO ENJOYS GARDENING. THE MOSS PAPER ON THE COVER MAKES A CLEVER FRAME FOR THE PICTURE OF A GARDEN, CUT FROM A GREETINGS CARD, WHILE THE PRETTY FLOWERS AND TINY GARDEN IMPLEMENTS ARE FROM A DOLL'S HOUSE SHOP. USING THE SAME BASIC DESIGN, THE THEME OF THIS BOOK COULD BE ADAPTED FOR A HOME IMPROVEMENT ENTHUSIAST, SUBSTITUTING A SUITABLE PICTURE FRAMED BY DOLL'S HOUSE BRICK-EFFECT WALLPAPER, AND ADDING A SET OF MINIATURE TOOLS.

1 Cut a piece of polyboard (foam board) 42 cm x 20 cm (16½ in x 8 in), and a piece of moss paper slightly larger. Mark two lines in the centre, 2.5 cm (1 in) apart, for the spine. Mark a square on the right-hand side of the polyboard for the picture and cut it out to make a window.

2 Partially cut through the polyboard on the spine. Remove the top layer of board and the foam with a knife.

3 Glue the moss paper to the front cover. Bend the board into a book shape then glue the moss paper to the spine and the back cover.

4 Glue the excess moss paper onto the inside, or stick down with double-sided carpet tape. Cut across the corners diagonally to reduce the bulk.

5 Make diagonal cuts in the moss paper from corner to corner of the window. Cut off most of this paper, fold the edges to the inside and stick down with glue or tape. Glue the picture, face down, behind the window.

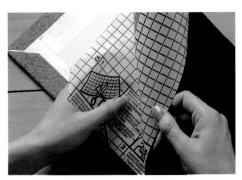

6 Cut a piece of sticky-backed felt to fit the inside of the board. Carefully remove the backing and stick the felt down, taking care not to crease it.

▶

MATERIALS AND EQUIPMENT YOU WILL NEED

CUTTING MAT • METAL RULER • CRAFT KNIFE • PENCIL • POLYBOARD (FOAM BOARD) • FLAT KNIFE • MOSS PAPER • PVA (WHITE) GLUE • DOUBLE-SIDED CARPET TAPE (OPTIONAL) • PICTURE OF A GARDEN • GREEN STICKY-BACKED FELT • BRADAWL (AWL) • DOLL'S HOUSE FLOWERS • MINIATURE GARDEN IMPLEMENTS • GREEN EMBROIDERY THREAD (FLOSS) • EMBROIDERY NEEDLE • THIMBLE • GOOD-QUALITY PLAIN WRITING PAPER • BONE FOLDER

7 Using a bradawl (awl), poke holes in the polyboard at the bottom of the window. Push the flower stalks in, applying a blob of glue to each stem beforehand.

9 Cut 21 sheets of plain writing paper and, using a bone folder, fold them in half. Lay them one inside the other in three sets of seven.

11 Each time you bring the needle out on to the spine, try and make the stitch straight and the same length as (and parallel to) the previous stitch.

8 Using embroidery thread (floss), stitch the miniature garden tools around the frame. Use a thimble to help you push the needle through the board.

10 Use the bradawl to make two holes in the fold of each set of pages, at an even distance from the top and bottom. Stitch each set of pages, starting from the inside and emerging on the spine.

12 Each time you return the needle to the inside, tie the ends of the thread in a neat bow.

CHRISTMAS ALBUM

PLAID CAKE BOARDS (AVAILABLE IN GOOD CATERING SHOPS DURING THE FESTIVE SEASON) ARE JOINED TOGETHER BY SIMPLE METAL SCREW POSTS (AVAILABLE IN CRAFT SHOPS) TO FORM THE COVER OF THIS FESTIVE ALBUM. A PAIR OF SCOTTIE DOGS, CUT FROM STICKY-BACKED FELT, COMPLEMENT THE THEME AND MAKE A CHARMING MOTIF FOR THE FRONT COVER. USE THIS BOOK WHEN PLANNING YOUR CHRISTMAS; THERE IS PLENTY OF ROOM FOR GUEST LISTS, SEATING PLANS, SPECIAL RECIPES AND GIFT IDEAS, AND AFTER THE FESTIVITIES IT IS THE PERFECT PLACE FOR CHRISTMAS MEMORABILIA SUCH AS PHOTOS OR CARDS.

1 Place the cake boards side by side and find the best position to join them (aim for an even distribution of pattern). Stick a 2 cm (¾ in) strip of double-sided carpet tape down both the edges to be joined.

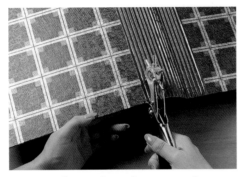

3 Line the inside with green sticky-backed felt. Make holes in the top and bottom of the back board, close to the edge of the cardboard, with a leather hole punch. Push a screw post into each hole.

5 Poke two holes with a pencil through the corrugated cardboard (avoiding the cake board) on the front cover side of the spine. Thread black tape through the holes and tie in a bow for decoration.

2 Cut a strip of corrugated cardboard about 11 x 25 cm (4 x 10 in). Stick this over the tape, joining the boards but allowing a small gap between them.

4 Cut 30 sheets of black card (cardboard) 24 cm (9½ in) square. Cut 30 card strips 4 x 24 cm (1½ x 9½ in). Make a hole gauge (see Basic Techniques) and punch out the holes in the card pages and strips. Slip them alternately on to the posts.

6 Make a template of a Scottie dog, and use this to cut out a black and a white felt dog. Cross a short length of narrow plaid ribbon at the neck of each dog and glue in position. ▶

MATERIALS AND EQUIPMENT YOU WILL NEED

2 PLAID FOIL CAKE BOARDS, 25 CM (10 IN) SQUARE • DOUBLE-SIDED CARPET TAPE • SCISSORS • METALLIC RED CORRUGATED CARDBOARD • STICKY-BACKED FELT: GREEN, BLACK AND WHITE • LEATHER HOLE PUNCH • 2 SCREW POSTS • BLACK CARD (CARDBOARD) • PENCIL • TRACING PAPER • BLACK COTTON TAPE • NARROW PLAID RIBBON • PVA (WHITE) GLUE • SELF-ADHESIVE BLACK CLOTH TAPE • BRADAWL (AWL) • 4 SPLIT PINS

7 Remove the backing from each dog. Stick the dogs on to the lower right corner of the front cover, so that the white one slightly overlaps the black one.

8 Cut a rectangle of self-adhesive black cloth tape to make a title plaque. At each corner, push a hole through the cloth, board and green felt using a bradawl (awl). Insert a split pin through each hole and open it up on the inside.

TRUSTY
FRIENDS

JEANS JOTTER

RECYCLE AN OLD PAIR OF JEANS BY COVERING A DULL RING BINDER FOLDER, TURNING IT INTO A COOL COLLEGE WORK BOOK. THE POCKETS ARE VERY HANDY FOR STORING PENS, PENCILS, ERASERS, SLIM NOTEBOOKS OR LETTERS. BUT REMEMBER, YOU CAN'T TOSS THESE JEANS INTO THE WASHING MACHINE! THIS PROJECT LOOKS COMPLICATED, BUT IT SIMPLY RELIES ON BASIC SEWING SKILLS AND PATIENCE IN ORDER TO ACHIEVE A REALLY GOOD "SKIN-TIGHT" FIT.

1 Cut the legs off the jeans and pick open the inside leg and crotch seams. Apply double-sided carpet tape all along the top edge of the folder.

3 Wrap the jeans around and slip-stitch all along the top edge, joining the front to the back. Then slip-stitch the two loose edges of denim on the inside to cover the folder completely.

5 Make darts on either side of the spine on the outside of the folder, as shown. It is important at this stage to try to keep the back seam straight and in the centre. This step can be a little tricky.

2 Align the back seam with the centre of the spine and stick the waistband to the tape, leaving the top edge slightly higher than the folder. Cut a seamless section from the cut-off leg and cut slits for the ring binders. Stick this to the inside of the folder with double-sided tape, folding a small hem top and bottom. Make sure the piece reaches the top and bottom edges.

4 Since the jeans will naturally flare out from the waistband, you will need to take up the extra denim by making darts at each side on the inside of the folder. Pin then slip-stitch the darts.

6 Fold under the excess denim at the bottom of the folder. Slip-stitch all along the bottom edge, joining the front to the back and also enclosing the folder completely.

MATERIALS AND EQUIPMENT YOU WILL NEED

PAIR OF OLD JEANS • SCISSORS • SEAM UNPICKER • RING BINDER FOLDER • DOUBLE-SIDED CARPET TAPE • SEWING NEEDLE AND MATCHING THREAD • DRESSMAKER'S PINS

WEDDING ALBUM

WHY NOT MAKE A WEDDING ALBUM AS ROMANTIC AS YOUR BRIDAL GOWN? LIKE THE GOWN, YOU WILL CHERISH IT FOR EVER, AND WHENEVER YOU LOOK AT IT YOU WILL BE REMINDED OF THAT SPECIAL DAY. THE COVERS OF THIS FLAMBOYANT ALBUM ARE MADE FROM STURDY SILVER CAKE BOARDS, THE FRONT COVER SMOTHERED IN SILK BLOOMS. INSIDE, THE ALBUM IS BOUND WITH SCREW POSTS (AVAILABLE FROM CRAFT SHOPS), ALLOWING YOU TO ADD OR REMOVE PAGES AS YOU WISH. WHEN YOUR WEDDING ALBUM IS COMPLETE, WRAP IT IN TISSUE PAPER AND LAY IT CAREFULLY IN A PRETTY HANDMADE OR STORE-BOUGHT BOX.

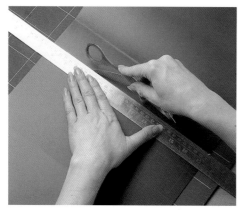

1 Cut a rectangle of polypropylene 30 x 65 cm (12 x 25½ in). Score two parallel lines, 5 cm (2 in) apart, across the mid-line, for the spine.

3 Using a punch and hammer, punch holes in the taped area on the back cover, near the spine, to correspond with the holes in the photographic refill pages.

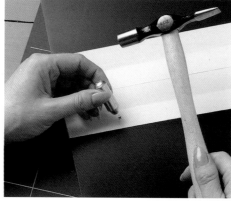

5 Cut the bulbous end from the base of the large flowers using sturdy scissors.

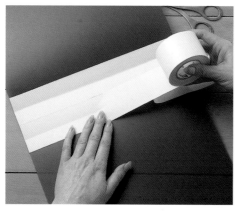

2 Reinforce the spine area on the inside using self-adhesive cloth tape.

4 Arrange the silk flowers on the front cover. Mark the position of the centre of each large flower.

6 Press a split pin through the hole in the centre of each large flower.

MATERIALS AND EQUIPMENT YOU WILL NEED

POLYPROPYLENE SHEET • CUTTING MAT • METAL RULER • 2 PAIRS OF SCISSORS, ONE VERY STURDY • SELF-ADHESIVE CLOTH TAPE • PUNCH • HAMMER • PHOTOGRAPHIC REFILL PAGES • ASSORTED SILK FLOWERS, LARGE AND SMALL • SPLIT PINS • CRAFT KNIFE • EPOXY GLUE • 2 M (2¼ YD) BROAD RIBBON • DOUBLE-SIDED CARPET TAPE • 3 SILVER CAKE BOARDS, EACH 30 CM (12 IN) SQUARE • WEIGHTS • 2 SCREW POSTS

7 Using a craft knife, cut a small slit at one of the marks indicating the flower positions on the front cover. Start at the centre and work outwards.

8 Take a large flower. Place your finger firmly on top of the split pin and push the ends through the slit.

9 Once the ends of the split pin are through the slit, open them up at the back. Repeat for the other large flowers.

10 Using epoxy glue, fill in the gaps by gluing on single petals here and there.

11 Glue smaller flowers all around the edge to hide the edge of the plastic.

12 Cut a length of ribbon long enough to wrap around the book and tie in a bow. Cut another piece to wrap over the spine. Lay the longer piece horizontally across the centre of the spine, then wrap the other piece around the spine. Attach both pieces using double-sided carpet tape.

▶

13 Punch holes in two of the cake boards to correspond with the holes in the back cover. Sandwich the polypropylene between the boards, silver side out, and glue together using epoxy glue. Weight the back boards until dry (see Basic Techniques).

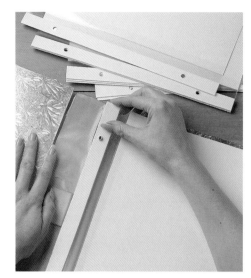

15 Insert the screw posts through the back cover, slip on the photographic refill pages and screw to secure. Tie the ribbon in a decorative bow to close the album.

14 Glue the front cover to the last cake board, with the ribbon sandwiched between and the silver facing out. Leave a narrow silver border around the edge. Let the back cover hang over the a table edge and weight the front cover, taking care not to damage the flowers.

ARCHIVE ALBUM

W HEN YOU DECIDE TO MAKE A PHOTOGRAPHIC ARCHIVE, CHOOSE CONSERVATION GRADE OR ACID-FREE CARD (CARDBOARD) FOR MOUNTING THE PHOTOGRAPHS AND ACID-FREE GLASSINE PAPER FOR PROTECTION. THESE TYPES OF CARD AND PAPER CAN BE BOUGHT IN SPECIALIST PAPER AND BOOKBINDING SUPPLIERS. BLACK-AND-WHITE PHOTOGRAPHS ARE MORE SUCCESSFUL IN THE LONG TERM THAN COLOUR PHOTOGRAPHS, AS THEY DON'T FADE AS QUICKLY.

1 Cut two rectangles of millboard (pasteboard) 22 x 31 cm (8¾ x 12⅛ in). Mark parallel lines 3.5 cm (1⅜ in) and 4 cm (1½ in) in from the spine edge. Cut the strips from each board, then replace them. Paste book cloth on to each board (see Basic Techniques). Remove each narrow strip, leaving a gap as shown.

2 Glue mull or bandage along the gap. Line the covers with decorative paper, pressing it into the gap using a bone folder.

3 Weight the covers while the glue is drying, to prevent warping (see Basic Techniques).

4 Using a leather hole punch, punch two holes about 2 cm (¾ in) in from the spine edge of each cover, and about 8 cm (3¹⁄₁₆ in) from the top and bottom edge.

5 Cut 20 pages of card (cardboard) 21 x 37 cm (8½ x 14⅝ in), and also 20 sheets of glassine 20 x 30 cm (8 x 12 in). Score parallel lines 3 cm (1¼ in) and 6 cm (2½ in) from the spine of the card pages. Fold the line nearest the edge and glue the flap. Insert the glassine and fold the card to the other line to secure.

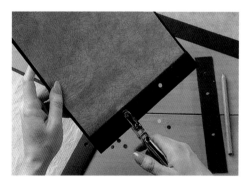

6 Make a hole gauge to match the covers (see Basic Techniques). Punch two holes in each card page. ▶

MATERIALS AND EQUIPMENT YOU WILL NEED

MILLBOARD (PASTEBOARD) • CUTTING BOARD • UTILITY KNIFE • CRAFT KNIFE • METAL RULER • PENCIL • PASTE (SEE BASIC TECHNIQUES) • BLACK BOOK CLOTH • SCISSORS • MULL, OR OPEN-WEAVE BANDAGE • DECORATIVE ENDPAPER • CONSERVATION PASTE • BONE FOLDER • WEIGHTS • LEATHER HOLE PUNCH • CONSERVATION GRADE, OR ACID-FREE BLACK CARD (CARDBOARD) • ACID-FREE GLASSINE PAPER • GLUE STICK • SCRAP PAPER • HOLE PUNCH • 2 BRASS SCREW POSTS • BLACK SELF-ADHESIVE CLOTH TAPE • PICTURE FOR FRONT PLAQUE • DOUBLE-SIDED CARPET TAPE

7 Push the screw posts into the holes in the back cover, then slip the pages and front cover on and screw together.

9 Cut off all the outer corners, leaving just enough overlap to be folded neatly back. Fold back the tape on the inside of the frame.

10 Cut out a picture or a card on which to write a name or title, to fit inside the frame. Stick to the back of the frame using double-sided carpet tape. Smooth with a bone folder.

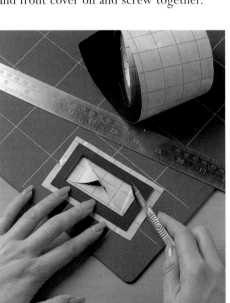

8 To make a front plaque for a name or picture, cut a card frame about 5 x 10 cm (2 x 4 in) and 1 cm (½ in) wide, and place it on a slightly larger piece of self-adhesive cloth tape. Make diagonal cuts from corner to corner.

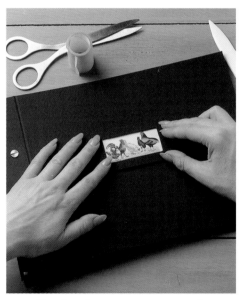

11 Fix the plaque in position on the front cover slightly above the centre, using double-sided carpet tape or glue.

COOKBOOK

USE THIS UNUSUAL SCRAPBOOK FOR YOUR FAVOURITE RECIPES, DINNER MENUS OR INTERESTING INFORMATION FROM LABELS OR FOOD PACKETS. BOTH THE BOOK COVERS AND PAGES ARE CUT FROM HANDMADE INDIAN KHADI PAPER, WHICH HAS A LOVELY TEXTURE AND A NATURAL DECKLE EDGE AND COMES IN VARIOUS COLOURS, AND THE BOOK IS BOUND JAPANESE-STYLE USING A WAXED LINEN THREAD. INSIDE, THE PAGE DIVIDERS ARE DECORATED WITH EMBOSSED FOIL MOTIFS PERTAINING TO THE DIFFERENT CATEGORIES OF FOOD: SOUP, SAVOURY DISHES, FISH OR POULTRY, VEGETABLES AND DESSERT.

1 Arrange the handmade paper with page dividers separating different colours. The sheets of card (cardboard) will form the covers.

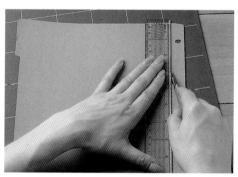

2 Using a ruler and craft knife, cut the punched edge off each of the page dividers and discard.

3 Using a bone folder, score a line 2 cm (¾ in) from the spine edge of each cover, page and page divider. Using a bradawl (awl) and a hole gauge (see Basic Techniques), make holes along this line at regular intervals.

4 Make templates of a variety of foods, cutlery and kitchen implements. Copy these on to tracing paper and tape to aluminium foil. Using a ballpoint pen, emboss the details on to the foil.

5 Using nail scissors, carefully snip out each embossed motif.

6 Cut a small rectangle of paper for each motif or group of motifs. Tear the edges against a ruler to give a deckle-edge effect. Glue each motif or group of motifs to its backing patch of paper. ▶

MATERIALS AND EQUIPMENT YOU WILL NEED

ASSORTED COLOURS OF KHADI OR ANY HANDMADE PAPER, A4 SIZE (8½ X 11 IN) • PAGE DIVIDERS •
2 SHEETS OF THIN CARD (CARDBOARD), A4 SIZE (8½ X 11 IN) • CUTTING MAT • RULER • CRAFT KNIFE • BONE FOLDER •
BRADAWL (AWL) • TRACING PAPER • MASKING TAPE • ALUMINIUM FOIL • BALLPOINT PEN • NAIL SCISSORS •
PVA (WHITE) GLUE • LINEN THREAD • NEEDLE • BEESWAX • 2 LARGE PAPER CLAMPS

7 Glue all the patches with food motifs to the first page divider, then write the names of the recipes alongside them. Alternatively, glue each on to a separate page divider. Glue the patches with "cutlery" motifs to the front cover. Collate the covers and pages.

8 Pull the linen thread through beeswax before you begin stitching (see Basic Techniques). Tie a knot on the inside near the spine at the bottom of the book.

9 Clamp the book firmly on either side to hold it in position while you bind it. Stitch the book in the Japanese style (see Basic Techniques).

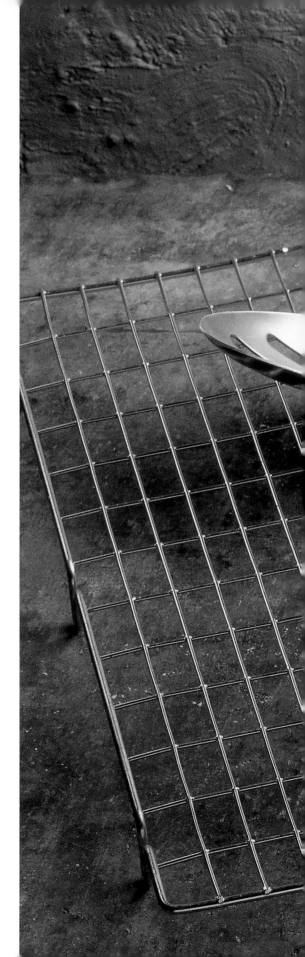

FRETWORK ALBUM

INSPIRED BY THE 19TH-CENTURY IRONWORK FOUND ON PIERS AND SEAFRONT BUILDINGS, THIS ALBUM IS IDEAL FOR DISPLAYING A COLLECTION OF OLD-FASHIONED SEASIDE POSTCARDS. THE "WROUGHT IRON" PATTERN IS CUT FROM PLYWOOD USING A FRET SAW, AND THE PAINT IS DISTRESSED TO ENHANCE THE NOSTALGIC FEEL OF THE DESIGN. CHEAP, TEXTURED, GREEN PAPER IS USED FOR THE PAGES, BUT YOU COULD ALSO USE CREAM-COLOURED CARD (CARDBOARD), WASHED WITH BLACK TEA TO GIVE IT AN ANTIQUE LOOK. ATTACH THE POSTCARDS TO THE PAGES WITH TRADITIONAL PHOTOGRAPHIC CORNERS IN BLACK OR BROWN.

1 From 4 mm (³⁄₁₆ in) plywood, cut two rectangles, one 16.5 x 19 cm (6½ x 7½ in) and one 17 x 22 cm (6¾ x 8¾ in) and one strip, 2 x 16.5 cm (¾ x 6½ in). From the 2 mm (¹⁄₁₆ in) MDF (medium density fiberboard), cut one strip 2 x 16.5 cm (¾ x 6½ in) and one rectangle 17 x 22 cm (6¾ x 8¾ in). Use a fretsaw or utility knife for this.

2 Glue the thin strips of MDF and plywood together and use masking tape to secure them until dry. Tape (but do not glue) together one ply rectangle and the MDF rectangle. Make a template of an ornate "wrought iron" frame and trace it on to the plywood side using a pencil.

3 Drill a starting hole at a convenient point on the pencil line of the design, to allow insertion of the fretsaw blade. Use the fretsaw to cut off the excess wood (shown as shaded areas) to make the basic shape only.

MATERIALS AND EQUIPMENT YOU WILL NEED

4 MM (³⁄₁₆ IN) PLYWOOD • 2 MM (¹⁄₁₆ IN) MDF (MEDIUM-DENSITY FIBERBOARD) • PENCIL • RULER • FRETSAW • UTILITY KNIFE (OPTIONAL) • PVA (WHITE) GLUE • MASKING TAPE • TRACING PAPER • "G"-CLAMP ("C"-CLAMP) • DRILL • SANDPAPER • WATERCOLOUR PAINTS: COBALT BLUE, BURNT UMBER, TURQUOISE, YELLOW, YELLOW OCHRE AND BURNT SIENNA • ARTIST'S PAINTBRUSH • RABBIT SKIN GLUE • WHITE EMULSION (LATEX) PAINT • BLOWTORCH • TELEPHONE DIRECTORY OR SIMILAR • IMPACT ADHESIVE • 2 SMALL HINGES • SMALL NAILS • HAMMER • GREEN PAPER OR CREAM CARD (CARDBOARD) FOR PAGES • HOLE PUNCH • POSTCARD OR PICTURE, FOR THE FRONT • NARROW RIBBON

4 Separate the two shaped pieces. Drill holes in all the enclosed, intricate shapes on the plywood, then cut them out using the fretsaw. Also cut out a border to fit within the main space. Smooth all the surfaces with sandpaper.

5 Remove the tape from the glued strips. Mark and drill two holes 8 cm (3 in) apart and 4.5 cm (1¾ in) from top and bottom. Make corresponding holes in the uncut ply rectangle (the back piece).

6 Mix together a little cobalt blue and burnt umber watercolour paint. Paint all the surfaces of the separate pieces and leave to dry.

7 Prepare the rabbit skin glue as directed on the packaging and dilute with water to a runny consistency. Paint a thin layer of glue over the front surfaces of the shaped pieces and strip, and the front and back of the back piece. Allow to dry thoroughly.

8 Paint the back panel, MDF strip and MDF front frame with white emulsion (latex) paint and, using a blow-torch, dry with a gentle flame until the paint cracks. Be careful not to burn the paint.

9 Mix equal quantities of turquoise and yellow watercolour paint with white emulsion to achieve a subtle colour. Paint the three pieces shown in the foreground. ▶

10 Mix a little yellow ochre and burnt sienna watercolour paint with water to get a thin wash and paint patches here and there to give an aged look. Be careful not to dislodge the "crackle".

11 Glue the tracery front and frame on to the backing MDF. Weight with a telephone directory or similar weight until the glue dries.

12 Lay the side strip alongside the front, with the tracery facing up. Mark 1 cm (½ in) from the top and bottom then glue hinges into place with impact adhesive. Drill little pilot holes for the nails. Snip the nails to size and gently hammer into place.

13 Cut pages and spacer strips to size and punch out holes to correspond with the cover. Glue a postcard or picture to the front page (make sure the cover frames it). Using ribbon, thread on first the back cover then the pages, alternating with the spacer strips, and finally the front cover. Tie the ribbon in a bow.

East Parade, Worthing.

PORTFOLIO

THE ADVANTAGE OF MAKING YOUR OWN PORTFOLIO IS THAT YOU CAN MAKE IT WHATEVER SIZE YOU NEED, AND YOU CAN COVER IT IN A FABRIC OF YOUR CHOICE. THE NATURAL-LOOK FABRIC USED HERE FOR THE COVER IS PRINTED WITH FEATHERS AND BIRDS' EGGS, AND COMPLEMENTS BEAUTIFULLY THE PLAIN CALICO

USED ON THE INSIDE. IRON-ON FUSIBLE (BONDING) WEB MAKES AN EASY OPTION FOR ATTACHING THE FABRIC, BUT FOR A MORE DURABLE, STRONGER METHOD YOU CAN MAKE YOUR OWN BOOK CLOTH BY GLUING A THIN PAPER BACKING TO FABRIC AND LEAVING IT TO DRY.

1 Using a utility knife, cut out all the pieces in the diagram from millboard (pasteboard). Trim off any rough edges and sand smooth.

2 Cut a piece of cover fabric (or book cloth and lining fabric) for each board. Then cut a piece of fusible bonding web for each piece of fabric. (If you are using book cloth, you will not need fusible web.)

3 Sandwich a piece of fusible bonding web between each board and its cover fabric, and iron to bond the fabric to the board. (Use glue if you are using book cloth.)

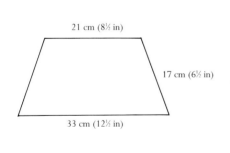

21 cm (8½ in)

17 cm (6½ in)

33 cm (12½ in)

x 2

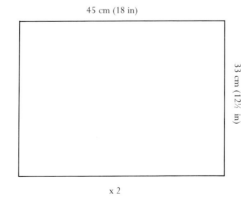

45 cm (18 in)

33 cm (12½ in)

x 2

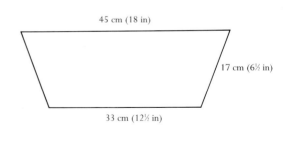

45 cm (18 in)

17 cm (6½ in)

33 cm (12½ in)

x 1

MATERIALS AND EQUIPMENT YOU WILL NEED

UTILITY KNIFE• MILLBOARD (PASTEBOARD) • CUTTING MAT • PENCIL • RULER • SANDPAPER • FABRIC FOR COVER, OR BOOK CLOTH • FUSIBLE BONDING WEB • CALICO FOR LINING • PEN • SCISSORS • IRON • 1 CM (½ IN) STRAIGHT-EDGE CHISEL • HAMMER • CRAFT KNIFE • NARROW LINEN TAPE, 2 LENGTHS EACH 50 CM (20 IN) • BRADAWL (AWL) • PVA (WHITE) GLUE • SELF-ADHESIVE CLOTH TAPE • BONE FOLDER

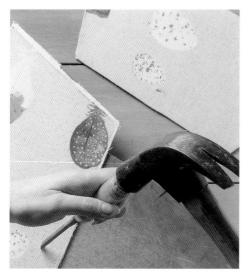

4 Midway along the inside edge of both short flaps on the cover side, about 2.5 cm (1 in) in from the edge, hammer a chisel in at an angle, to make a slot.

6 Use a bradawl (awl) to push the linen tape through the slot from the cover.

8 Using fusible web as before, iron lining fabric on to each piece of board. (Use glue if using book cloth.) The lining will hide the tape in the recess on the short flaps.

5 Working on the reverse side and using a craft knife, carefully remove a thin channel of board below the slot, to make a recess the width of the linen tape.

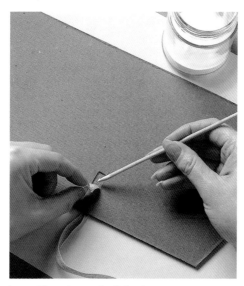

7 Glue the end of the linen tape into the recess on the reverse side and leave to dry.

9 Using self-adhesive cloth tape, tape the side and top edges of the front cover board, and reinforce the bottom corners of both cover boards. Allowing a 2.5 cm (1 in) gap between the edges of the boards, join the bottom edges with a strip of tape on both sides (the tape acts as a hinge).

▶

10 Tape the side and top edges of the two short flaps and one long flap. You may find it easier to stick the tape to one side all along the edge, then fold it over the edge and secure it on the other side.

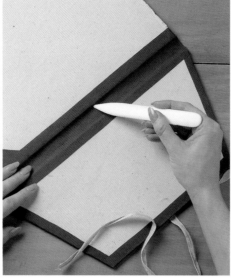

12 Run a bone folder along the taped joins (seams) to give definition and to ensure that the tape is firmly stuck. Smooth out any creases in the tape.

11 Tape the bottom edges of the short flaps to the side edges of the back cover, using a strip of tape on both sides and leaving a 2.5 cm (1 in) gap between the edges of the boards as before.

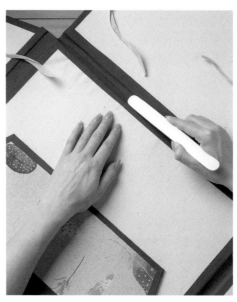

13 Tape the bottom edge of the long flap to the top edge of the back cover as before. Finally, run over all of the taped joins with a bone folder, to ensure good bondage.

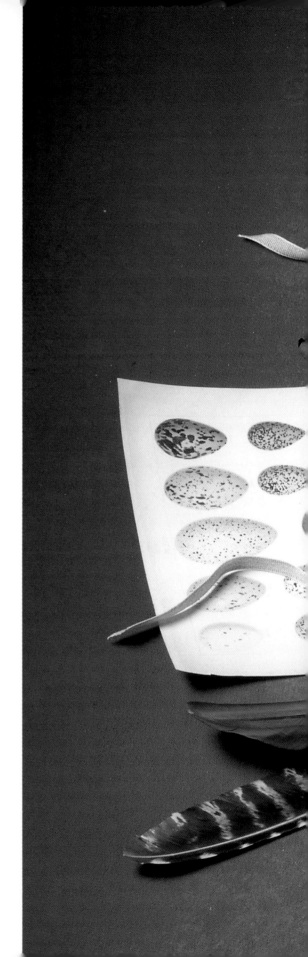

SCENTED CHRISTENING BOOK

Delicately scented drawer lining paper comes in very pretty patterns and is delightful for a special occasion book. As a practical alternative to individual cards, ask the christening guests to write in it their special messages for your child. Use papers in soft tones and choose silk ribbon to complement your colour scheme. Deckle-edge the pages and arrange them in order of size to achieve a pleasing petal effect. For the finishing touch, frame a photo of your baby or a Victorian scrap picture on the front cover.

1 Cut a piece of polyboard (foam board) 65 x 29 cm (26 x 11½ in). Mark two parallel lines across the centre, 1.5 cm (⅝ in) apart. Partially cut through the polyboard (see Basic Techniques) along the lines, to form the spine.

2 Bend the polyboard into a book shape. Paste drawer lining paper on to the board (see Basic Techniques), making sure that you fit the paper right into the cut lines.

3 Line the inside of the cover using the same paper. Leave to dry under a couple of telephone directories to prevent warping. Mark the position of two holes on the back board, about 7.5 cm (3 in) apart and 2.5 cm (1 in) from the spine. Use a sharp pencil to punch the holes.

MATERIALS AND EQUIPMENT YOU WILL NEED

POLYBOARD (FOAM BOARD) • CUTTING MAT • CRAFT KNIFE • METAL RULER • PASTE (SEE BASIC TECHNIQUES) • BONE FOLDER • SCENTED DRAWER LINING PAPER • TELEPHONE DIRECTORIES • SHARP PENCIL • WADDING (BATTING) • PAPER OR FABRIC LACE • SQUARE OR RECTANGULAR DOILY • DOUBLE-SIDED CARPET TAPE • GLUE STICK • BABY PHOTOGRAPH OR VICTORIAN SCRAP PICTURE • SCISSORS • NARROW SILK RIBBON • ASSORTED DECKLE-EDGED SCISSORS • ASSORTED PASTEL-COLOURED PAPER • SCRAP PAPER • HOLE PUNCH

4 With the tip of the pencil protruding through the hole on the inside, trim the rough edges of the hole using a craft knife.

6 Use double-sided carpet tape to stick first the wadding, then the paper and finally the lace to the centre of the front cover.

8 Cut two pieces of ribbon about 5 cm (2 in) longer than the entire cover, and two about 5 cm (2 in) longer than the spine. Run the glue stick along the ribbons before sticking them down along the cover on the outside, about 2 cm (¾ in) from the edge. The ribbons should cross at the corners and end on the inside.

5 Cut same-size rectangles of paper, wadding (batting) and lace. Cut the decorative border off a doily. Choose patterns and textures to suit the cover drawer lining paper.

7 Using a glue stick, fix the doily border around the edge of the lace to make a frame. Glue a photograph or Victorian scrap picture on to the lace, in the centre of the frame.

9 Cut two pieces of ribbon just shorter than the spine. Glue them inside the front and back covers so that they hide the ends of the ribbons which extend over from the front.

▶

10 Using various deckle-edged scissors, cut sheets of paper, each one slightly smaller than the last. Make one sheet 4 cm (1½ in) longer than the others.

12 Working from the back, thread the ribbon through the holes in the cover. Next, thread the long sheet on, just through the holes in the page (lift the flap out of the way). Thread all the pages on, in decreasing size order, and, lastly, thread the ribbon through the holes in the flap from the long back page. Tie the ribbon in a bow and trim the ends at an angle.

11 Make a hole gauge (see Basic Techniques) and punch two evenly spaced holes near a narrow edge of each sheet. Using a bone folder, score and fold the extra-long sheet 4 cm (1½ in) from one narrow edge. Using the hole gauge as a guide, punch two holes through both layers of paper.

TRIANGULAR BOOK

THIS BOOK PRESENTS A REWARDING CHALLENGE FOR THE MORE EXPERIENCED BOOKBINDER. IT HAS A STYLISH AND CONTEMPORARY LOOK AND ITS SHAPE SUGGESTS THAT IT BE USED WHERE CONVENTIONS NEED TO BE BROKEN DOWN. NOVELTY SHAPES FOR BOOKS ARE NOT A MODERN PHENOMENON — IN THE NATIONALE BIBLIOTHÈQUE IN PARIS THERE IS A BEAUTIFUL HEART-SHAPED ILLUMINATED MANUSCRIPT, DATING FROM MEDIEVAL TIMES, WHICH CONTAINS LOVE SONGS. WHEN YOU SET ABOUT DESIGNING A SHAPE FOR A BOOK, CONSIDER THE PURPOSE OF THE BOOK AND CHOOSE THE SHAPE ACCORDINGLY.

1 Cut 18 sheets of good-quality writing paper into diamond shapes, with all the edges measuring 21.5 cm (8½ in). Fold them in half to make two equilateral triangles. Group into six sets of three.

2 Make a "W" fold (see All-in-One Stitching, Basic Techniques) in a diamond-shaped sheet of textured paper and glue to one of the folded sheets of writing paper. Remove all but a 4 cm (1½ in) margin along the spine edge of the purple paper and the underside. This is the "wasted edge". Make another the same. Stitch the sets of pages together, following the instructions in steps 3–6 of All-in-One Stitching, Basic Techniques.

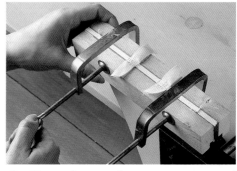

3 Clamp the spine between two strips of wood. Apply PVA (white) glue along the spine, lay a strip of mull or bandage along the spine and apply more glue over the top.

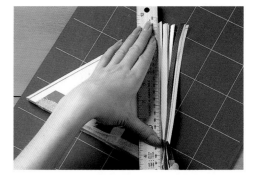

4 Place the book on a cutting mat and, pressing firmly, trim the uneven edges of the pages against a metal ruler, using a utility knife. You may need to make repeated cuts to get through the pages.

MATERIALS AND EQUIPMENT YOU WILL NEED
METAL RULER • SCISSORS • WHITE OR CREAM GOOD-QUALITY WRITING PAPER • CHEAP, TEXTURED, CREAM PAPER • PVA (WHITE) GLUE • UTILITY KNIFE • LINEN TAPE, OR SEAM BINDING • VICE AND CLAMPS • 2 STRIPS OF WOOD • MULL, OR OPEN-WEAVE BANDAGE • CUTTING MAT • STIFF CARDBOARD OR MILLBOARD (PASTEBOARD)• SCRAP OF THIN CARD (CARDBOARD) • SILK EMBROIDERY THREADS (FLOSSES) • GOLD PAPER • PASTE (SEE BASIC TECHNIQUES) • BLACK BOOK CLOTH • CIRCLE CUTTER (CUTTING COMPASS) OR CRAFT KNIFE • BONE FOLDER

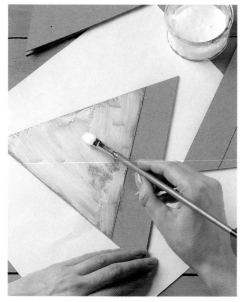

5 Cut four equilateral triangles from cardboard or millboard (pasteboard), 22.5 cm (8¾ in). Draw a 4 cm (1½ in) margin on one side of each. Glue together in pairs, leaving the margin edges unglued.

7 To make a fancy end tab, curl the end of a strip of card (cardboard) 1 x 4 cm (½ x 1½ in) and glue then wrap silk threads over the curl. Make two tabs, and glue one at each end of the spine, so that the curl projects over the pages.

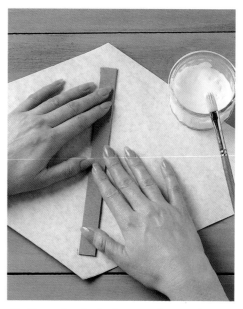

9 From book cloth, cut a diamond 2.5 cm (1 in) larger all round than the paper diamonds in step 1. Cut a strip of board exactly the length of the spine. Glue the strip exactly in the mid-line on the paper side of the book cloth.

6 Apply glue to both sides of a purple "wasted edge" and slide it between a pair of boards at their unglued margins. Repeat to make the second cover.

8 Cut two pieces of gold paper to fit the covers exactly. Paste on to the covers and smooth out any bubbles.

10 Fold the book cloth around the book and press around the edges with your fingertips to transfer the outline to the book cloth. ▶

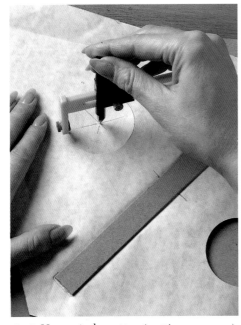

11 Use a circle cutter (cutting compass) or template and craft knife to remove a 5 cm (2 in) diameter circle from both sides of cloth.

12 Trace the circle on to the gold covers. Apply glue to the gold back cover, carefully avoiding the circle. Smooth the book cloth in position. Repeat for the front cover.

13 Use a bone folder to smooth over the covers, eliminating any air pockets. Work outwards from the circle.

14 Using a bone folder, tuck in the book cloth at the top and bottom of the spine.

15 Glue along the overlapping edges of the book cloth, fold in and smooth over with a bone folder.

16 Glue the end pages in place inside the front and back covers, and smooth in place.

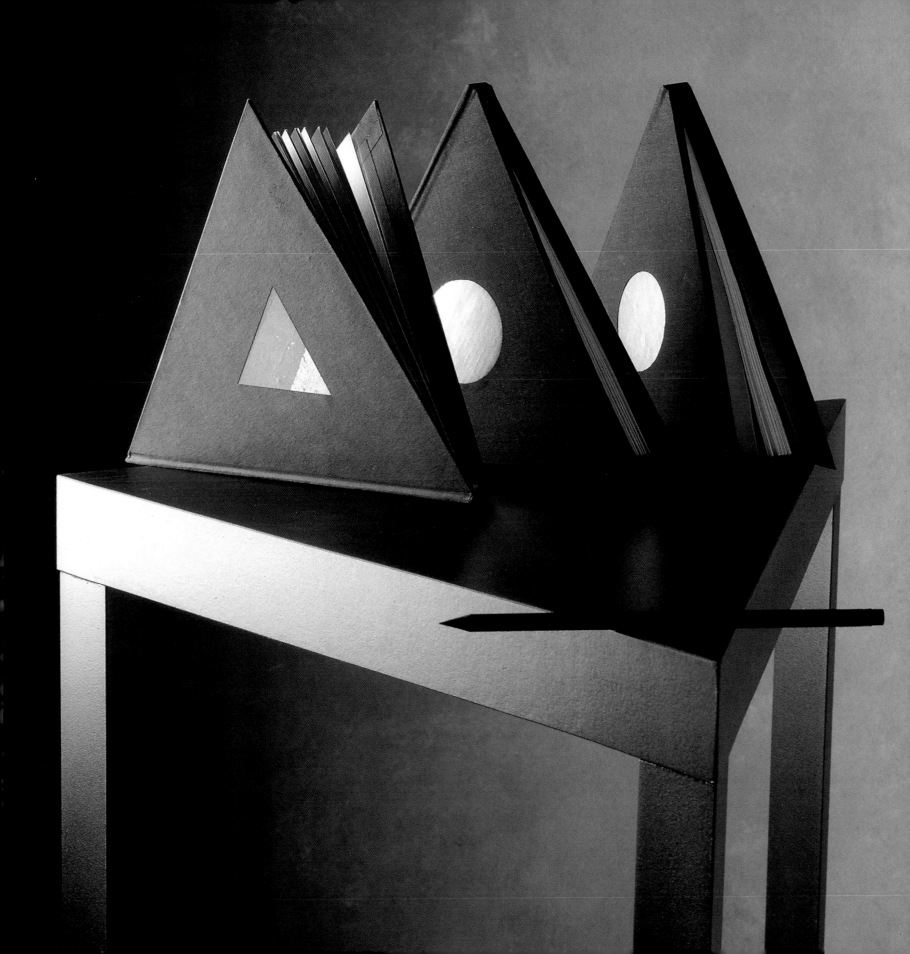

CLASSIC NOTEBOOK

THIS CLASSIC BOOK MAKES A PRACTICAL GIFT FOR THE BUDDING WRITER. ITS LINED PAGES ARE TAKEN FROM AN ORDINARY EXERCISE BOOK AND ARE STITCHED TOGETHER USING THE ALL-IN-ONE METHOD. READYMADE BOOK CLOTH IS AVAILABLE FROM SPECIALIST SUPPLIERS, BUT YOU CAN EASILY MAKE YOUR OWN BY LINING YOUR CHOICE OF FABRIC WITH A THIN SHEET OF PAPER. SIMPLY CUT THE PAPER LARGER THAN THE FABRIC, SPREAD PVA (WHITE) GLUE ON TO THE PAPER AND WAIT UNTIL IT BECOMES TACKY. THEN PLACE THE FABRIC, RIGHT SIDE UP, ON TO THE GLUED PAPER, SMOOTH OUT ANY AIR BUBBLES AND ALLOW TO DRY.

1 Remove the staples from the 16 x 20 cm (6¼ x 8 in) exercise book(s) and carefully take out the folded pages. Group them into six sets, laying the pages one inside the other. Make a hole gauge (see Basic Techniques) and make holes in each set of pages using a bradawl (awl).

2 Make a "W" fold in two 16 x 20 cm (6¼ x 8 in) sheets of lined paper (see All-in-One Stitching, Basic Techniques). Cut two endpaper sheets to size and glue them to the outside edge of a "W".

3 Using the bradawl, make holes to correspond with the holes in the pages. Using a needle and long thread, stitch the sections together (see steps 3–6, All-in-One Stitching, Basic Techniques).

4 Clamp the spine of the book between two strips of wood, and slip two strips of linen tape or seam binding under the stitching, across the spine. Glue a 17 x 3 cm (6¾ x 1¼ in) strip of mull along the spine (see step 8, All-in-One Stitching, Basic Techniques).

MATERIALS AND EQUIPMENT YOU WILL NEED

1-2 STANDARD EXERCISE BOOKS • SCRAP PAPER • PENCIL • METAL RULER • BRADAWL (AWL) • LINED PAPER • ENDPAPER • SCISSORS • PVA (WHITE) GLUE • NEEDLE • WAXED LINEN THREAD • VICE AND CLAMPS • 2 STRIPS OF WOOD • LINEN TAPE OR SEAM BINDING • MULL OR OPEN-WEAVE BANDAGE • CUTTING MAT • UTILITY KNIFE • CARDBOARD OR MOUNT BOARD • THIN CARD (CARDBOARD) • SILK EMBROIDERY THREADS (FLOSSES) • BOOK CLOTH • BONE FOLDER

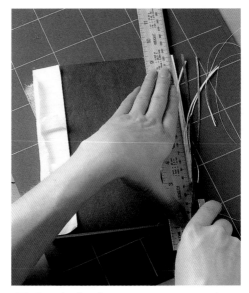

5 Lay the book on a cutting mat and, pressing firmly, trim the pages against a metal ruler using a utility knife.

6 Cut four 21.5 x 16.5 (8½ x 6½ in) sheets of cardboard or mount board, leaving a 5 cm (2 in) margin at the edge of each. Glue together in pairs, leaving the margin edges unglued.

7 Apply glue to both sides of one "wasted edge" (see All-in-One Stitching, Basic Techniques) and slide it between a pair of boards at their unglued margins. Repeat to make the second cover.

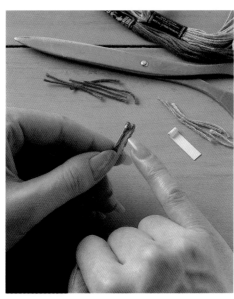

8 Make two fancy end tabs by curling and gluing two 0.5 x 3 cm (¼ x 1¼ in) strips of thin card (cardboard), and wrapping silk threads over the curl. Glue flat against the top and bottom of the spine, so that the curls project over the pages.

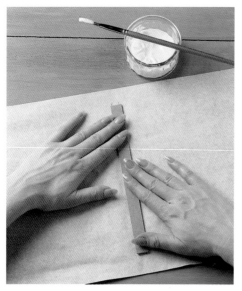

9 Cut a rectangle of book cloth and a strip of board the exact length of the spine. Glue the strip exactly in the mid-line on the paper side of the book cloth.

10 Position the book on top of the book cloth and cover it completely with glue.

▶

11 Fold the book cloth over the front cover and smooth with a bone folder, working from the spine outwards. Repeat with the back cover.

13 Using a bone folder or similar, tuck in the book cloth overlap at the top and bottom of the spine.

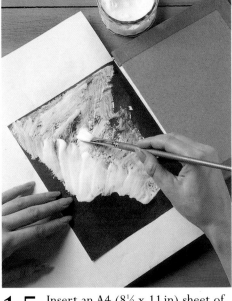

15 Insert an A4 (8½ x 11 in) sheet of paper under the endpaper at the back. Spread the endpaper with glue.

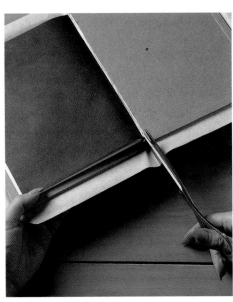

12 Trim off the corners of the book cloth, leaving an overlap the width of the cover board. Using a sharp pair of scissors, cut slits in the "wasted edge" to correspond with the edges of the spine, taking care not to cut the book cloth.

14 Stand the book on its spine and support it in that position. Open the front cover and glue down first the top and bottom overlaps, then the side overlaps. Repeat for the back cover.

16 Smooth the endpaper in place on the inside back cover, using a bone folder to eliminate any air pockets. Repeat steps 15 and 16 for the front cover.

June 1959] ALTERNATIVE MATHEMATICS

$\sin. \frac{B}{A}$

JAPANESE STORK ALBUM

JAPANESE BINDING IS DECEPTIVELY EASY TO DO AND, ALTHOUGH IT LOOKS DELICATE, IT IS SURPRISINGLY STRONG AND SECURE. FOR THIS ALBUM THE STITCHING "THREAD" IS A SOFT, PLAITED STRING AND, SINCE IT IS TOO THICK TO THREAD ON A NEEDLE, A LOOP OF WIRE IS TWISTED AROUND IT TO ACT AS A GUIDE. THE COVER IS MADE FROM A MOTTLED HANDMADE PAPER, DECORATED WITH A STORK MOTIF. YOU MAY PREFER TO DESIGN YOUR OWN MOTIF TO COMPLEMENT THE THEME OF THE CONTENTS, WHETHER THEY ARE PHOTOGRAPHS, POSTCARDS, LETTERS OR MEMORABILIA.

1 From cardboard cut two rectangles 30 x 33 cm (12 x 13 in) and two strips 30 x 3.5 cm (12 x 1⅜ in). Lay each strip beside each rectangle, with a slight gap between. Paste a strip of mull or bandage along the join.

3 Cut two sheets of contrasting paper to line the cover, ideally using a rotary cutting blade. From card (cardboard) cut 26 pages 29.7 x 36 cm (11¾ x 14¼ in) and 27 pages the same size from the glassine paper.

5 Cut strips of card 4 cm (1½ in) wide, to fit the scored margins. Using a glue stick, glue a strip to each page.

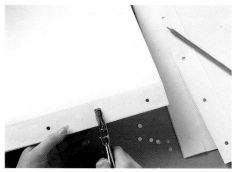

6 Using a hole punch, punch four holes at equal intervals in each of these pages. Do the same with the glassine sheets. ▶

2 Cut the paper for the cover, allowing a 2 cm (¾ in) overlap. Paste on the paper (see Basic Techniques). Turn the board over, trim the corners and paste the edges back neatly.

4 Using a bone folder, score a line on each sheet of card, 4 cm (1½ in) in from the spine edge.

MATERIALS AND EQUIPMENT YOU WILL NEED

CARDBOARD • CUTTING MAT • CRAFT KNIFE • METAL RULER • MULL, OR OPEN-WEAVE BANDAGE • HANDMADE PAPER • PASTE (SEE BASIC TECHNIQUES) • HANDMADE PAPER IN CONTRASTING COLOUR • ROTARY CUTTING BLADE (OPTIONAL) • CREAM CARD (CARDBOARD) • GLASSINE PAPER • BONE FOLDER • GLUE STICK • HOLE PUNCH • SCISSORS • PLAITED STRING • BRADAWL (AWL) • PVA (WHITE) GLUE • THIN WIRE • SILVER FOIL • GRASSES AND STRAW • SCRAP PAPER • WEIGHTS

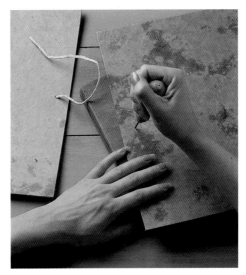

7 Cut two lengths of string 25 cm (10 in). Working from the front, make a hole with a bradawl (awl) in the front and back cover, halfway down and close to one narrow edge. Push each string through the holes from the front. Glue the frayed ends on to the inside.

9 Collate the pages, alternating card pages with glassine paper pages. Cut a strip of cover paper wide enough and long enough to fit over the spine. Fold the ends over as shown. (It may help to first apply a little glue to the spine with a glue stick.)

11 Use silver foil, grasses, straw and scraps of torn, handmade paper to decorate a plaque for the front of the album. Make a simple stork image or create your own design.

8 Glue the lining paper on to the inside of the covers, hiding the ends of the string. Pierce holes on the spine edge of each cover board to correspond with the holes in the pages.

10 Loop a piece of thin wire around a long length of string and twist the ends together to act as a needle. Bind the book in the Japanese style (see Basic Techniques), but here, because the string is bulky, tie the knot on the outside.

12 Glue the plaque in the centre of the front cover. Place a piece of scrap paper on the front of the book and weight the book until the glue is dry.

SUPPLIERS & ACKNOWLEDGEMENTS

ACKNOWLEDGEMENTS

The author and publishers would like to thank the following artists for the projects and gallery pieces photographed in this book:
Susan Allix p15
Clare Andrews p72–75
Penny Boylan p69–71
Marcus Davies p84–91
Timothy C. Ely p14
Evangelia Biza p15
Heidrun Guest p92–94
Susan Johanknecht p12, 14
Peter Jones p14
Trevor Jones p12, 13, 15
Gavin Rookledge p13
Philip Smith p13–15

PICTURE CREDITS

The publishers would like to thank the following for permission to reproduce pictures in this book:
p8, Victoria and Albert Museum; p9, The British Library (top and bottom); p10, The British Library (top), The British Library/Bridgeman Art Library (bottom); p11, The British Library (top), Christie's Images, UK/Bridgeman Art Library (bottom).

SUPPLIERS

Listed here are a few addresses of specialist shops:

UNITED KINGDOM

Falkiner Fine Papers
76 Southampton Row
London WC1B 4AR
Tel: 0171 831 1151

Khadi Papers
Unit 3
Chilgrove Farm
Chichester
West Sussex PO18 9HU
Tel: 01243 535314

Paperchase
213 Tottenham Court Road
London W1P 9AF
Tel: 0171 580 8496

Shepherds Bookbinders Ltd
76 Rochester Row
London SW1P 1JU
Tel: 0171 630 1184

USA

Colophon Book Arts Supply
3611 Ryan Road, S.E.
Lacey, WA 98503
www.the gridnet/colophon

Fascinating Folds
P.O. Box 10070
Glendale, AZ 85318
Tel: (800) 968 2418
www.fascinating-folds.com

Jerry's Artarama
P.O Box 58638J
Raleigh, NC 27658
Tel: (800) 827 8478
www.jerryscatalogue.com

Nasco Arts and Crafts
4825 Stoddard Road
Modesto, CA 95397
Tel: (800) 558 9595
www.nascofa.com

Twinrocker Handmade Paper
100 East 3rd Street
Brookston, IN 47923
Tel: (800) 757 8946
www.twinrock.com

AUSTRALIA

A to Z Art Supplies
50 Brunswick Terrace
Wynn Vale, SA 5127
Tel: (08) 8289 1202

Art & Craft Warehouse
19 Main Street
Pialba, QLD 4655
Tel: (07) 4124 2581

Artland
272 Moggill Road
Indooroopilly, QLD 4068
Tel: (07) 3878 5536
Free call: 1800 81 5377

Bondi Road Art Supplies
181 Bondi Road
Bondi, NSW 2026
Tel: (02) 9386 1779

Eckersleys
126 Commercial Road
Prahran, VIC 3181
Tel: (03) 9510 1418

Janet's Art Supplies & Books
145 Victoria Avenue
Chatswood, NSW 2067
Tel: (02) 9417 8572

Jacksons Drawing Supplies
Hay Street
Perth, WA 6000
Tel: (08) 9321 8707

Oxford Art Supplies Pty Ltd
223 Oxford Street
Darlinghurst, NSW 2010
Tel: (02) 9360 4066

INDEX